PILGRIM'S
NOTEBOOK

PILGRIM'S NOTEBOOK

An Experience
of Religious Life

David A. Fleming, S.M.

ORBIS BOOKS

Maryknoll, New York 10545

The Catholic Foreign Mission Society of America (Maryknoll) recruits and trains people for overseas missionary service. Through Orbis Books, Maryknoll aims to foster the international dialogue that is essential to mission. The books published, however, reflect the opinions of their authors and are not meant to represent the official position of the society.

Copyright © 1992 by David A. Fleming

Published by Orbis Books, Maryknoll, NY 10545
Printed in the United States of America

Library of Congress Cataloging-in-Publication Data

Fleming, David A.
    Pilgrim's notebook : an experience of religious
life / David A. Fleming.
        p.   cm.
    ISBN 0-88344-754-1 (pbk.)
    1. Monastic and religious life.   I. Title.
BX2435.F55   1992
255 – dc20   91-21488
                                                                      CIP

TABLE OF CONTENTS

ACKNOWLEDGMENTS

I am indebted to the Rev. Christie Joachimpillai, O.M.I., for initial insights, given orally some fifteen years ago, that have since evolved in my own mind into the analysis of the meaning of "religious life" presented in Chapter 1.

I am also grateful to my friend Brendan Keevey, C.P., for a number of rich suggestions about mission that I've developed in Chapter 6. His thoughts were included in a letter on ministry addressed to the members of his religious province in the United States.

The analysis of predominant mindsets common among religious developed in Chapter 2 was heavily influenced by the seminal work of Thomas E. Clarke, S.J., in a variety of essays and lectures.

INTRODUCTION

A MATRIX OF REFLECTION

One morning, when I was in my middle teens, I woke with an overpowering conviction that life in a religious community was the path to which God was calling me and the one that I myself wanted.

This conviction was not the culmination of any conscious reflective process. Nor would I call it a mystical experience. No doubt it was in its way a logical outcome of a long process of Catholic education, the example of sisters and priests whom I admired, and an anguished adolescent search for identity and meaning. I can recognize that preparatory process now, but at the time the intuitive conviction simply burst upon me, without analytical consciousness.

I wanted to be a religious* in some order, preferably one in which I could be a brother rather than take on the cultic and pastoral tasks of the priest. Strangely enough I had never met

---

*To speak of "religious life" and to use the noun "religious" as we do in the Roman Catholic Church, referring to organized and recognized celibate communities and their members, is faulty terminology. It seems to restrict the religious dimension — something that belongs to all people — to a small elite.

Yet no other brief phrases are at hand as generic terms for the many different varieties of these communities. With some tinge of regret I will therefore use these long-traditional terms throughout this book.

1

a brother before; my desire for this way of life was more the result of an intuitive inner logic than the aspiration to imitate any specific person.

A much admired sister-teacher helped me to examine a number of communities of religious brothers. With relative ease my choice fell upon the Marianists. I had not heard of them previously, but the way they expressed their self-understanding gripped me. Within a few months I had entered their training program.

In time my initial disinclination for priestly ministry disappeared, and with sympathetic encouragement and flexible Marianist structures, I eventually became a priest in a congregation composed of a majority of brothers.

My story of vocation is certainly atypical. It is more like the vocation stories of the Marianists I now live with in India than those of most of my American confreres.

I don't tell this story, however, because I think it is in any way a norm; in fact, psychoanalysts would perhaps discover worrisome tendencies in it. Over the years my motivation has greatly evolved and my sense of vocation has known many twists and turns. I only evoke the story of my initial vocational experience at the beginning of this book because the intuitive sense of the rightness of religious life for me has been a personal constant through a variety of experiences and modes of explanation, and because my readers should rightly know the particular kind of experience from which I speak.

For I hope this will be the kind of book that speaks from and to experience. As I prepare the Orbis edition of my pilgrim's notes, I hope my experiences as a "religious" may strike themes of interest to laypersons Catholic and Protestant.

I think of contemporary religious as a "we," not a "they." My desire is to reflect from honestly faced reality on the meaning of our journey as Roman Catholic religious today. I do not want to produce a theoretical treatise or speak from a priori abstractions or from wishful thinking, no matter how lovely these may seem. (Too often, alas, a priori abstractions and wishful thinking greatly resemble each other!)

Perhaps this book, which has grown out of my experience, will evoke and illuminate the experience of others.

The thirty-some years that have passed since that initial experience of call have been marked in our religious communities by an extraordinary process of change. The era of transformation through which we are passing shows no signs yet of coming to a conclusion. The process of corporate change parallels and externalizes the personal growth and change so many of us have experienced in this latter half of the twentieth century. Like most religious, I have identified with the image of the "pilgrim" as I moved over the years through so many way-stations of experience and spirituality.

These are notes jotted down along the way. My experience, my personal life-context, its breadth and its limitation, will condition their validity.

Now I find myself at work as a director of novices in the Indian subcontinent, witnessing another and particularly vital form of religious life today within a culture radically different from those in which I have previously lived. I have long felt an affinity with the religious life (Christian, Hindu, Buddhist) of South Asia, and have immersed myself for some years in reading and study that have eased this transition. I feel very much at home here, both accepted and accepting in a revitalizing way. Institutionally and numerically at least, religious life is in decline in the other places where I have worked; here it is rapidly growing for reasons that, after all is said and done, remain somewhat mysterious to me. This Asian component of my experience will certainly be evident to the reader.

This notebook of pilgrim jottings has been enriched by each step along the way. I am also aware of the limits this same background imposes. Like most reflections on its topic, this book has its time and its place, straddled somewhere between Asia and North America in the last years of the twentieth century.

CHAPTER 1

RELIGIOUS LIFE AND
THE HUMAN CONDITION

Since Vatican II most of us religious have felt the need to emphasize the bonds we share with others, our common humanity. The accent has shifted from "separation from the world" to creative involvement in it. We hope to contribute to the transformation of this earth, to the coming of God's reign in our human space and time. Many of us reject signs of separateness that once seemed holy and styles of life that contrast too sharply with those of ordinary people. Whether this thrust is successful or not, right-minded or not, its aim is to erase any sense of strangeness and irrelevance about religious life and bear witness to a full-hearted involvement in what Vatican II calls the "joys and sorrows, the hopes and aspirations" of the people of our times.

Despite these aspirations for integral humanity, too often we still act and speak as if our religious life were a phenomenon that grows solely from Christian sources of revelation or from ecclesiastical history in Europe. The truth is that the religious life as we know it in the Catholic church is one instance of a worldwide phenomenon among people of faith.

Living in the Kathmandu valley, at a conflux of the religious energies of Asia, I am constantly surrounded by reminders that our Christian religious life is an instance of a wider human

5

impulse. Wandering Hindu *sadhus* call at our gate and pass me on the street, a quiet smile often on their faces, pursuing a form of religious life not often seen in Europe since the days of St. Benedict, who had a Roman distaste for an unorganized and wandering lifestyle. Buddhist monks, who seem like us to be at a turning point in their history, inhabit neat, often newly built establishments and distinguish themselves by gentle friendliness.

Almost everywhere we go in the world of religion, once cultures attain a certain level of economic, social, and spiritual development, we find the emergence of some form of communally organized "monastic" life comparable to Catholic religious communities. The ashrams and maths of Hinduism, the Sufi brotherhoods of Islam, the *sangha*, which is the core of Buddhist life, perhaps even the Hassidic communities of Judaism—all these are instances of a similar impulse in the religious striving of the human race. Some cultures and theologies are more hospitable to such religious communities (for example, Catholic Christianity and all forms of Buddhism), while others (for example, Protestantism, Islam, and Judaism) are more reticent and cautious in regard to them.

This widespread and varied "religious life" is, first of all, a form of "life." To call something a life is to define it in dynamic, not static, terms. Life is a process. It always involves birth, growth, maturity, decline, and death. In human life this process also involves consciousness: striving, satisfaction, conflict, joy, passion, and the two irreducible instincts Freud identified as *eros* (love) and *thanatos* (death).

Our human life unfolds as we search to fulfill needs and desires for such goods as food, clothing, shelter, physical and psychological well-being, relaxation, rest, transportation, employment, acceptance, and information. The pursuit of such needs and wants seems endless because the satisfaction of one need frees energy to pursue another. Eventually our restless human striving may even focus attention on a need for ultimate meaning and transcendence.

Our identity as human persons evolves as we take up a stance, find a place, within each of these three spheres. Hindu religious thought has integrated something very similar to these spheres into its understanding by the doctrine of the "human aims" or *purusharthas*, each of which has its own legitimacy and sacred meaning within life. We may take *artha* (wealth) as equivalent to the "economic sphere" and *kama* (pleasure) as equivalent to what we are calling the "domestic sphere." *Dharma* (sacred duty within the human community) has many affinities with what we are calling the "political sphere." In the Hindu doctrine, these three aims of life are eventually transcended in the fourth and final *purushartha, moksha* ("salvation" or "liberation").

As Christians, in following the path of "religious life," we are of course not exempt from human striving in these three domains, though we, like the devout Hindu, desire liberation from anxious craving for illusory happiness. As religious persons we seek a religious meaning in the activities of each of these three basic spheres.

THE ECONOMIC SPHERE:
SANNYASA AND HUMAN PRODUCTIVITY

Every human person establishes some kind of relationship to the subhuman world, the world which in the story of Genesis was given over to human rule and domination. Universally people tend to measure success in life by this relationship: What do I achieve in the economic sphere? How thorough is my domination of the surrounding material world? How much wealth do I control? Is the quality of my domination beneficent or evil, enslaving or freeing? Whether we are concerned with immense economic endeavors or simply the husbanding of minimal necessities, in corporate board rooms and in minor personal decisions, we are economic beings.

In religious terms the economic sphere is usually recognized as a gift from God but also as an arena of temptation. We are prone to abuse nature, to grasp it greedily for ourselves. Thus we disfigure and pervert it, distorting the primordial harmony of the whole of creation. We are also tempted to enslave others and even ourselves to the subhuman forces of the material world. These temptations are the root of the crises of the economic sphere today: ecological destruction, mindless consumerism, self-centered manipulation, and unjust distribution of goods.

The economic sphere is a focus of religious teaching and ideals. Taoism teaches harmony with nature; Islam emphasizes the rigorous duty to share wealth with those less fortunate; for many traditional religions whose roots are lost in prehistory, the earth itself is sacred. Every religion offers its characteristic guidance, its unique spirituality of the earth. Christian saints and thinkers bear a varied witness to the economic implications of the teaching of Jesus — think, for instance, of Francis or Calvin or Teilhard.

It is not only Catholic religious orders that seek to observe a "holy poverty." Communities of religious life in all traditions propound an ideal in the economic sphere for their members. The *sannyasa* of Hindu and Buddhist monks is a renunciation of striving for economic achievement and security. This renunciation is often far more rigorous than that of Christian religious, for it may even forego a fixed abode and any assurance of one's daily bread. As in Christian religious communities, this renunciation only makes sense as an approach to a reality greater and deeper than the economic sphere.

There is a very widespread kind of religious logic, apparent in traditions of all kinds, which leads some people to withdraw from natural and legitimate forms of economic activity with the aim of attaining a new level of inner freedom and spiritual depth. Today religious poverty has come to the forefront of our agendas in Catholic religious communities, for we are seeking not only a deeper spirituality in a materialistic world, but also a closer identification with the majority of the human race, which lives in conditions of poverty and even *sannyasa*, not from religious choice but from grim and unjust necessity.

THE DOMESTIC SPHERE: *BRAHMACARYA* AND HUMAN INTIMACY

We also establish personal identity through intimacy with other human beings and with ourselves. In such intimacy we create for ourselves a name, a home, and a progeny. In the intimate, domestic sphere partners profoundly affect their mutual destinies and those of their children. Success in life is often measured in terms of intimate relationships: What kind of companions do I have and what do I mean to them? Whom do I know and how well? How do I relate to myself and my own body? Are my human and intimate relationships freeing or somehow enslaving? Living a celibate life is one of many ways of living with and for others.

Human beings are tempted to pervert human relationships, to manipulate them for selfish ends, and ultimately to isolate themselves from the power of authentic love, from other persons, and from their own bodies. In such isolation life becomes miserable for oneself and also, often, for one's companions. It is then that "hell is other people," as the characters discover in Sartre's *No Exit.*

Today's crisis of the intimate domain is expressed in the prevalence of problems of identity and sexuality, in the widespread striving for liberation of women, in the redefining of roles and stereotypes, and in the much heightened expectation of personal satisfaction and experiential fulfillment in relationships. Many dimensions of this crisis are surely signs of growth; yet the intimate, domestic domain is a key arena of suffering, in human history but very especially in our times.

Religious traditions present a variety of ideals for the domestic sphere. Hindu teaching in this domain is especially prolific, including the stories of the Ramayana, the laws of Manu about familial and communal duty, the doctrine of the *ashramas* or stages of life, the Vedantic reflection on the true *atman*, the self and its relationship to all that exists, and much else besides. Ancient Greek and Roman religion presented ideals of passionless self-conquest (Stoicism) and profound self-knowledge (Platonism). Islamic law details the God-ordained relationships and mutual duties that govern the domestic sphere. Buddhist, Chinese, and Jewish heritages offer rich guidance as well. In Christianity the teaching and example of Jesus lead to a whole order of intimate relationships based on *agape*, selfless love.

Human instinct seems to be evolving toward greater personalism, and few of these traditional ideals seem unambiguously satisfying or all-encompassing today. This fact complicates but does not nullify the effort on the part of religious in all these traditions to consecrate their energies in the sphere of intimacy.

In Sufism and in some forms of Buddhist monastic life children and family are allowed, but the primary intimate commitment of the monk or dervish remains to the circle of disciples. In Catholic Christianity and in religions born in India this consecration usually takes the form of celibacy (*brahmacarya*). Celibacy may be embraced for a lifetime (as is normative in institutionalized forms of religious life) or for a special period (the first and last *ashramas* in the classic Hindu pattern). Celibacy is life-denying, not life-enhancing, and therefore antireligious, unless it leads to a rich form of love and self-gift to others. Its purpose is to probe to an intimacy with God that overflows in spiritual availability to many.

Whatever the precise form of the consecration, those of us who pursue any organized form of special religious commitment seek to find a deeper meaning, one that links us to the foundation of life itself, in the sphere of intimate relationships.

THE POLITICAL SPHERE:
GURUS, DISCIPLES AND HUMAN POWER

We also attain identity and purpose in human life through our association with other persons to engage in the pursuit of common meanings and to attain common ends of work, defense, and welfare. This is the "political" sphere in the broadest sense of the word, for it concerns relationships within human society (the "polis"). Life's achievements are measured by standards drawn from this domain: How much power do I have over others? How much corporate effort can I harness? How much of a contribution do I make to society? How influential am I in determining corporate directions? This sphere is as real in religious communities as in houses of parliament.

Of course the political sphere is also a realm of temptation. We are consistently in danger of perverting our political power, which can enable us to serve and contribute to the common good, into a force for selfish domination. We all too easily, almost unconsciously, seek to focus the energies of society upon the attainment of our own selfish desires. Such are the corrupting demons of human power. The endemic crisis of power in government and institutions today attests to the activity of these demonic impulses.

Power, its use and abuse, is a key focus of religious reflection everywhere. Figures as diverse as Moses and Ashoka, Confucius and Muhammad, Mahatma Gandhi and Dag Hammerskjold, manifest something of the range of religious ideals for the political sphere.

Members of religious communities in the various traditions seek to consecrate this sphere by the voluntary acceptance of experienced spiritual guidance. Thus they hope to be purified from illusions and from the self-centered use of power in order to attain a compassionate, nonviolent, loving, and community-enhancing servanthood.

Sufis define their allegiance by long lineages of spiritual guides, so that the initiate in the Sufi brotherhood can trace his masters back to the early days of Islamic spirituality. Consecration of the sphere of power is expressed in Hinduism and Buddhism through fidelity as a disciple (*chela*) to a wise spiritual master (*guru*). In Christianity this consecration once took an almost identical form, in the days of the Fathers of the Desert who served as spiritual masters; today such discipleship has been institutionalized in the vow of obedience.

Whatever form the religious ideal may take in the political sphere, it is impossible for us to be authentically religious persons without some commitment of energies for the right use of power and freedom. In today's world, characterized at once by greater means of power and greater feelings of powerlessness than ever before, this commitment grips us as religious persons very deeply.

WHAT MAKES LIFE "RELIGIOUS"?

We can be religious only in terms of our time and place. A human life may be qualified as "religious" when it seeks to express in terms of a given culture the deepest meaning, the transcendent thrust, of the basic life-impulses just described.

The religious dimension of culture is already evident in the word itself: it is derived from *cultus*, the Latin word for "worship." The arts and sciences, philosophy and history within any given civilization normally originate in a supportive role for worship.

It would not be going far beyond the evidence to say that the humanization of life has always focussed, at least at the origin of a civilization, on the effort to establish a right relation with the deepest meaning of life, that is, on the religious quest. Conversely, it has generally seemed to most people, at most times and places, impossible to be religious without deep involvement in one's culture.

Yet as religious persons we stand, today as always, in a paradoxical relationship to culture. We both proclaim God's presence and denounce God's absence in our time and place. Inevitably we issue a judgment on the validity of cultural expressions, accepting some as authentic in the quest for attaining the end of human existence, rejecting others as mere illusion or temptation. Religious figures regularly condemn fascination with objects unworthy of rightly ordered human life, regularly warn against attaching an illusory permanence to passing and ultimately unsatisfying manifestations of human achievement.

In the opening chapters of the history of the Jewish people, we find Moses demanding Pharaoh to "let my people go so that they may worship God on the mountain" — an appropriate symbol for the way in which captivity in the economic, intimate, and political spheres misdirects or prevents the release of the religious energies implicit in culture.

Similarly, the great temptation narratives of religious history warn against fascination with goods that are illusory or inadequate. The children of Israel in the desert must forget their hankering for the "fleshpots of Egypt." In the *Bhagavad Gita* Arjuna learns from Lord Krishna how to perform one's duty without being ensnared by a passion for results. Jesus triumphs over temptations to distort his ministry in order to ensure worldly success. The Buddha attains enlightenment only after rejecting the comforts of princely privilege and a variety of false paths to liberation. St. Antony of the Desert, the first celebrated Christian "religious," struggles with demons for years before becoming, unintentionally, the spiritual father of a great religious movement. Authentic religious life in our time as well is a struggle against today's demons and temptations.

In fact, a witness frequently characteristic of any life that is religious is the struggle with the perverting demonic energies that deflect all spheres of human life from their true purpose. The religious person is one who fights the demonic (the evil, ugly, and unreal — that which is the opposite of the good, beautiful, and true) in all spheres of human culture: work, politics, sexuality, and the rest. There is no genuine religious life without this struggle. In this time of rapid cultural change we experience the struggle in a particularly acute fashion.

Because of this ongoing struggle with the demonic, the religious person normally does not find a comfortable and well-adjusted place in life. The nonreligious forces of culture, those that ignore the pursuit of ultimate meaning, attempt to humanize life through an "adjustment" to "reality." Most of the time these forces of specious adjustment dominate society.

Thus the religious person is typically drawn to those who are marginal to human society. He or she is not easily domesticated by existing societal arrangements, not even ecclesiastical ones. The religious person lives "on the boundary," in solidarity with those who share this marginality: the young, the old, the poor, and the sick. To focus on the rich and successful is normally a flight from vocation for the religious person. This fact has become much more alive in our consciousness during the past two decades.

A certain marginality is a not surprising consequence of a life devoted to the pursuit of meanings deeper than those canonized by conventional wisdom. Rather than accepting the compromises which close society in on itself, the religious person characteristically searches for transcendence, for deeper, unexpected meanings. The Upanishads and the literature of Buddhism are full of paradoxical tales and statements which show that the path to wisdom and redemption requires a going apart from convention. Muhammad and his followers are free only after an *hegira* from familiar settings and an entrance into the new social fabric of Medina. The Virgin Mary discovers a new meaning in Isaiah 7:14: "a maiden shall conceive." The prophet constantly asks, "Is there any word from the Lord?" Hosea discovers God's loving kindness even in his relationship with a faithless wife. While the rest of his people are content with dancing around the golden calf, Moses experiences the revelation of Sinai. Religious today are especially gripped by the face of God in the victimized of society and in those who stray outside conventions and norms: the poor and the homeless, drug addicts and AIDS victims, lepers and battered women.

Since this attitude stretches human capacity, the religious person very often experiences "temptation." He or she leaves behind some of the normal ways of life that soften human ambiguities and inadequacies. It is easy to mistake a false demonic attraction for the voice of God. Freely choosing the unconventional and doing direct battle with the demonic is hazardous. One does so only out of a fascination with "what eye has not seen, and ear not heard, nor has entered into the human heart."

A person who succeeds in conquering the demonic within human experience and culture becomes a gracious presence to others, witnessing to the harmonious direction of all to the true good of human existence. Thus the greatest saints of all religions are those who have attained the deepest humanization.

Such a person comes to a new appreciation of riches which seemed lost. He or she becomes intoxicated with new ways of possessing (Francis of Assisi), relating (Gandhi), and exercising power (the Boddhisattva). This person is able to mourn and yet feel there is nothing to mourn for, enjoy life even if there seems to be nothing to laugh about, do commerce in penury, and deal with the world without becoming engrossed in it. The religious person lives fully in this world and simultaneously transcends it (cf. 1 Cor 7:29-31). This dialectic of involvement and transcendence pervades all forms of religious experience, not only Christianity. It is especially challenging in our time of cultural transformation.

Thus religion occupies a paradoxical place within human life. At the heart of life in its pursuit of humanization, religious experience is never able to settle down within the structures of normal living but breaks through these in pursuit of deeper meanings. Religious experience may be described as a process of ever-deepening penetration beyond the surface of life and into its core.

The foregoing thoughts may be helpful in reflecting on the widely shared impulse, mentioned above, to emphasize the full humanity of this form of life. By thinking of our Catholic religious communities within the context of universal religious experience, we can better understand and evaluate current trends and find the basis for a sympathetic but thoroughgoing critique of recent traditions and practices. This mindset can free us, embolden us for the new departures which seem necessary in our times. It can also foster a sensitivity for the radicality of the impulse which is at the core of every genuine religious vocation, and for our kinship with those who seek holiness in all traditions.

CHAPTER 2

AN UNFINISHED HISTORY

This is a book of notes and musings on experience, but it would be narrowing to confine our reflection to what one person may know or feel. Time and again reflection on the history of religious life has enlightened and invigorated my perspectives with the light of other times and other places, other mentalities and sensibilities. In this chapter I will recall some major paradigms of the past and survey those that now seem current. I hope that reflection on the changing modes of being religious will give some depth and breadth to our understanding and perhaps a bit of encouragement and consolation to our experience of the present, unsettled era.

Throughout its long history Christian religious life has evolved greatly, regularly producing new forms, ideal types, and organizing principles. It appears that this mode of life is today in the throes of giving birth to a new, still not fully developed paradigm for self-understanding.

The cultural context for religious life in the Roman Catholic Church has been European and, during the past two centuries, increasingly North American. In other parts of the world this form of life has been transplanted and modelled on these predominant cultural forms. It is in these two closely linked geographical areas that communities of religious life today are feeling the most intense stress and pressure for transformation, the most painful premonitions of death of old forms.

We have seen that religious life, if it is authentically lived, tends toward a concomitant immersion in culture and prophetic tension with it. Exemplary religious have typically been deeply involved people who bring a challenging sensitivity based on the gospel to the issues of their age. The great moments in the history of religious life are those in which this prophetic marginality has been most evident, fueling imagination and idealism. The sad moments are those when critical involvement has been replaced by safe distancing, and prophetic tension has given way to comfortable accommodation, when religious have become so well-adjusted that they simply support a status quo, or so abstracted from the world that they appear to their contemporaries merely irrelevant or curious.

HISTORICAL FORMS OF RELIGIOUS LIFE:
A BIRD'S-EYE VIEW

The historical evolution of Christian religious life is well-known and documented (for example, see Raymond Hostie, S.J., *Vie et mort des ordres religieux* [Paris: Desclée de Brouwer, 1972], and Lawrence Cada, S.M., *Shaping the Coming Age of Religious Life* [New York: Seabury, 1979]). Here we can simply allude to the principal key currents in order to illustrate the variety and wealth of ways of thinking about religious life through a long history, perhaps occasionally to startle us by an unexpected but liberating viewpoint.

In the fourth century the unique life of the Fathers and Mothers of the Desert, like St. Antony and St. Mary of Egypt, captured Christian imagination. Their movement was born out of a deep concern to keep alive the radical nature of the Christian message. Taking on many of the philosophic and ascetic currents of their age, they protested by their very way of life against the domestication of Christianity that followed on the Constantinian establishment. They left behind an imperial culture that they judged to be Christian in name but not in attitude and pursued a new, heroic form of seeking God alone in solitude and asceticism. In their lifestyle and often in their spirituality, they were more like the wandering *sadhus* of India today than like any current Christian form of religious life.

The life of the desert ascetics called several generations of Christians away from a worldly religiosity and developed a profound current of Christian mysticism. Yet in its aberrations this mode of life easily led to mere eccentricity and spiritual hoboism.

So it was that, before very long, stable communities with an organized and guided life developed. Saints Basil and Benedict eventually became recognized as the great legislators for this pattern of religious life. In time, monasteries and convents became great feudal families, creating an alternative to the brutal environment of early medieval Europe. Within this environment prayer, learning, hospitality, peace, and order could be cultivated amid a world of ignorance, war, and chaos. This monastic mode of life regularly experienced reform movements aimed at presenting a more genuine religious witness within a slowly changing culture. In spirituality and lifestyle this monastic mode, which still flourishes within Eastern and Western Christianity, is much akin to Hindu and Buddhist monasticism today.

With the rise of bourgeois culture in the High Middle Ages, many felt the need for a new way of being religious within the city, and not behind monastic walls. So there appeared a new religious paradigm—that of the *fraticello*, the little brother (Franciscan, Dominican, Carmelite, or other)—who sought to be in fellowship with all and to serve the spiritual and material needs of a new kind of human community. In a world increasingly dominated by materialism, consumerism, and heterodox religious enthusiasm, the friars sought to bear witness to simplicity, poverty, and sound religious teaching. In many ways their form of religious life resembled that of Islamic Sufi communities, which took shape about the same time.

The life of the friars—so visible and open to large numbers of people, devoted to so high a spiritual aspiration, and existing in an increasingly critical and reform-minded society—was inevitably vulnerable to accusations of hypocrisy and infidelity. The mendicant way of life remained controversial throughout the late Middle Ages, sometimes pilloried for succumbing to distracting worldly beguilements, sometimes attacked for the very radicality of its ideals.

The challenge of the Reformation and the obvious need for church renewal in the sixteenth century gave rise to a new form of religious life, principally congregations of priests (Jesuits, Piarists, Oratorians, and many others), who emphasized total dedication to the needs of a threatened church. Disciplined and well-trained for mission, the Clerks Regular aimed to take the spiritual offensive in the great post-Tridentine plan to counter heresy, renew the life and discipline of the church, and spread the gospel to parts of the world that were newly known and still untouched by European Christianity. Unified and centralized, these groups sought to propagate a purified, educated, clerically centered, devout, and self-confident Catholicism. Communities of women also sought to take up this paradigm for religious life, but they consistently met obstacles in a society that tended to disapprove of any substantial role for women in public life.

The activist orientation of this mode of religious life naturally evoked opposition, and the passionate involvement of the members in the culture of their time easily led to questionable alliances with worldly power. Yet it was less internal decline than hostile external force which led to the rapid eclipse of this form of religious life in the late eighteenth and early nineteenth centuries. The French Revolution, the Napoleonic era, hostile "enlightened" regimes in countries as diverse as Portugal and Austria—all conspired to suppress all forms of religious life indiscriminately.

The equally rapid restoration and the rise of new forms of religious life from 1810 to 1870 is remarkable. In an effort to restore a tradition that had been suppressed, the new or refounded religious congregations once again modified the paradigm of their lives, structuring it around the project of building a network of church institutions for education, health care, social service, and missionary proclamation. Apostolic congregations of religious women finally came into their own. The democratic spirit of the times, together with demographic explosion, called for a great expansion of church institutions, and religious pioneered in providing services which were only later offered by secular agencies. The meaning of religious life took on a new richness as women and men both expressed their faith commitment in pragmatic and often daring ventures to meet urgent societal needs.

Parallels with the last two forms of Christian religious life are infrequent in other world religions. The more mission-minded congregations have flourished in the activist conditions of modern Western civilization. These congregations are much influenced by the spirit of Reformation and Enlightenment—a historical mood which has only lightly marked the experience of other world religions.

After more than 150 years the post-French-Revolution form of religious life, too, has begun to lose some of its luster. Other agencies compete with religious to serve needs for education, health care, and social welfare, often with more impressive means. A certain routine has overtaken many religious foundations, and the understanding of religious life has not kept pace with the intellectual currents of the age. In the popular mind religious often seem well-meaning but irrelevant, somehow antiquated.

Of course this overview of history is neither exhaustive nor nuanced. Yet I believe it is accurate in delineating the major paradigms that have appeared in religious life up to the present.

PARADIGMS FOR TODAY

Some decry the "death of religious life" in our times, but it seems unlikely that so fundamental and long-lasting a strand of Christian life will simply disappear. Of course it may take dramatically new forms and attract a far different proportion of Christians than formerly. It seems clear that the time has come for the emergence of new patterns of religious life, which will be as different from past forms as each of those just described has differed from what preceded it. The new forms, if they are to succeed, will have to respond, in both affirmation and prophetic protest, to the cultural circumstances of our times.

What will the new forms be? The answer is not easy. The emergence of new paradigms today is all the more difficult because it is happening simultaneously with major cultural shifts, in a world characterized by competing habits of thought and feeling that vie for approval. Classic, modern, and post-modern cultures coexist, often side by side. There is no unitary contemporary culture that provides a firm soil for the implantation of a new mode of religious life.

Thus, in the search for new vitality, current-day religious experience a tension among varied cultural outlooks and mentalities. It will be helpful to sketch three of the predominant mindsets common among religious and explore their implications (see also, Thomas E. Clarke, S.J., "Religious Leadership in a Time of Cultural Change," *Religious Life at the Crossroads*, ed. David A. Fleming, S.M. [New York: Paulist Press, 1985], pp. 168-89).

THE CLASSICAL VIEW

We may call the first of these mentalities the classical view. This outlook takes a static, non-evolutionary, hierarchically ordered approach to life. In this view religious life is a fixed "state of perfection" in the church, clearly contrasting with the secular state of life. Religious life is a higher way, following the evangelical counsels, in contrast with the way of the commandments followed by seculars. Religious are supposed to be separated from the world, alien to secular concerns. Sacrality, hierarchical order, and fixed essences characterize this mode of thought. It conjures up for many of us an image of the self-contained and isolated motherhouses in which we were trained. In many ways this mentality remains a "fall-back" culture, away from which we have moved rather definitively, but against which we still measure change. It is the best articulated understanding of religious life available to us, since it has been well-formulated in numerous popular manuals. It is reinforced by political, social, artistic, and religious sensibilities of large numbers of people in society in general: those who long for the "restoration" of a stable and harmonious order and are attracted by many conservative evangelists and political leaders.

We often feel severe dichotomies between experience and this traditional ideal. Even though most of us no longer affirm this classical mentality, we sometimes hark back to it with quite a bit of nostalgia and no little guilt.

A MODERN VIEW

Especially during the past forty years the classical synthesis within the Roman Catholic Church has been severely challenged by modern culture. In politics, art, and economics, this modern view has been dominant since the Enlightenment. It takes an optimistic view of human possibilities, a liberal and individualistic approach to societal improvement and exalts the capacity of the modern person to reform the world in the name of progress.

When applied to religious life the modern culture emphasizes mission. It aims to update religious life in order to make it more adaptable to the contemporary world and more effective in the services it offers. Without envisioning a thoroughgoing transformation of lifestyle, this view emphasizes a pragmatic adaptation to apostolic needs.

In this modern view religious are bands of Christians who come together mainly for the purpose of getting a job done (whether the "job" is education, health care, evangelization, or even contemplation), as well as for some level of mutual support. Self-reliance and the cultivation of individual gifts are highly prized. Individual freedom and participative governance are obvious corollaries, within the content of a shared sense of mission.

The core of this modern way of understanding religious life is an attempt to relate in a positive way with the world of today. The modern mode implies a "theology of the world" that affirms creation as issuing forth from the hands of God, progressing toward the realization of God's reign. The world is seen as a relatively autonomous reality which can evolve and advance on its own and thus make its unique contribution to the life of the church and the unfolding presence of the Spirit in history.

Like any paradigm, this modern conception presents its own pitfalls. The modern stance has not been effective in helping us take a critical consciousness toward the dark side of the world in which we live. It is as if we emerged from a Jansenistic negative evaluation of the world into a naive overemphasis on its beauties and goodness and a blindness to its dark sides. Appreciation of creation easily degenerates into consumerism. Personalism sometimes becomes individualism: narcissistic focus on one's own sensitivities, feelings, and personal development, without much attention to the realities of people beyond oneself or to a corporate response to their needs.

With its positive and negative sides, I believe that this is the dominant outlook of most of us religious today. This outlook is surprisingly common to all age groups. Differences among us tend to be differences about how to accommodate in a more positive way to the modern world—not differences which call into question the desire to accommodate.

A POST-MODERN VIEW

Some religious, however, have instinctively moved on to another view. The post-modern outlook which underlies their thought implies a critique of the liberal optimism that stems from the Enlightenment. Without wishing a reactionary return to the classical synthesis, post-modern thought calls for a more radical transformation of society, with great emphasis on community and solidarity. Less optimistic and more critical than the modern mentality, post-modern ways of thought have gained much ground in the second half of this century. Proponents of the post-modern outlook are the "radicals" and the transforming "outsiders" in the fields of politics, art, economics, and culture.

For religious who take this approach, religious life is seen not as a state but as an historically changing path of discipleship. It is understood as an explication of baptismal vows that are shared in common with all Christians. All elitism is excluded, even the elitism of professional service. The aim is to be close to the local church and in touch with the people, in solidarity with them, rather than to act upon them in a professional form of ministry. This vision gravitates around qualifiers like "holistic," "comprehensive," and "integrating."

Keynotes of this paradigm are solidarity and interdependence — the desire to allow ourselves to be influenced by others and to join with them in discernment of the common good. The walls between religious and lay Christians are de-emphasized. Some accuse this attitude of being merely a form of secularism. However, religious who adopt this view see themselves as pilgrims and prophets, collaborators with other people in building up God's reign. They aspire to be signs of unity, dialogue, and simplicity in a world that puts little value on these ideals.

In Latin America this paradigm gives rise to small religious communities living among the poor and stimulating the development of "basic Christian communities." In India the same model prompts religious to establish ashrams that live a life very close to that of the rural poor and to adopt prayer styles and life-rhythms congenial to the Indian heritage. In North America and Europe the post-modern view leads to the establishment of communities in normal urban living quarters, where the religious share rhythms of life and work with their neighbors.

This vision for religious life remains tentative and exploratory, and few would claim to incarnate it fully. It tends to be more fully actualized in the Third World than in the First. Yet it is an ever clearer aspiration of many religious, seeming to spring up almost simultaneously in many different cultures and areas of the world.

THE PARADIGMS AND RELIGIOUS COMMUNITY

To clarify in less abstract terms the interplay and tension within religious life among these divergent mentalities and paradigms, it will be helpful to see how they are at work in contemporary debates on community.

The classical model relates community to spiritual discipline. This model sees a religious community as a structure to aid individual and corporate asceticism. In this view life together in community is an important element in religious consecration and a stimulus for individual holiness. Accountability to the local superior, fidelity to the common rule and timetable of the community, and the use of goods as a community rather than as an individual — all are ways of overcoming self-centeredness, facilitating the life of prayer and the apostolate, and leading to a commitment beyond self-will. The community maintains a stance of separation from the world. Large numbers of members are often helpful to maintain the structure of community life, which is a good in itself.

A major value underlying this view is the recognition of the need for discipline, structure, and authority in order to deepen spirituality. This model is particularly well-adapted to a corporate apostolate staffed by all or most of the members of the community. The sense of corporateness is strong in lifestyle and in apostolic work, even if there are tensions and resentments. This model tended to predominate in the period between Vatican I and Vatican II, although during that period groups founded for an apostolic purpose often lived a life much closer to the second model.

The modern view relates community to mission. This model views community primarily as a band of ministers in mission. Community life is structured in function of the common mission to be achieved by the members of the community. Relationships among the members focus on the fulfillment of this mission. The superior is seen as a team leader, or at least as an animator for the mission. The structures of community life are highly adaptable in function of the needs of the mission. The community sees itself in service to the world, seeking "to be in the world but not of it." The size of the community may be large or small, depending on the needs of the mission. Frequency and intensity of mutual relationships among members and the structuring of community activities are handled flexibly in terms of the mission to be accomplished. Physical presence and regular community gatherings are valued only to the extent that they assist the community in accomplishing its mission. Exceptions are readily made when the mission seems to warrant them. Living together in the same religious house can sometimes be sacrificed when apostolic needs seem to demand it, but in such cases efforts are made to link members living in scattered places so that they will have a corporate sense of mission.

The major value in this model is its emphasis on creativity and flexibility in attaining the mission of the community and the church. Efficiency in giving genuine service to the people of God is likewise stressed. This approach to community can facilitate the work of all the members in a single apostolate but it is also viable for communities that are engaged in a variety of tasks, provided they recognize some common focus in their mission. If teamwork within the mission is working well, the sense of corporateness can be very strong; otherwise, it suffers.

The post-modern view sees community in terms of relationship; the community is a focal point for relationships among people. We manifest and build God's kingdom and the church through such relationships. The quality of community is gauged principally by the level of dialogue among the members, their relationship to the local church around them, and their ability to support, challenge, and enrich one another. The superior or coordinator is a focus of unity and dialogue within the group and with those in its environment. Because of the great concern for individual gifts and talents, this style of community tends to be quite flexible in regard to timetable and other structures, including common life under the same roof, provided there is a high level of interaction among the members. Smaller numbers seem most desirable in such a setting. This paradigm also emphasizes dialogue and relational solidarity with the local church and the immediate neighborhood. Such a community aims to be an incarnational presence, a witness to God's reign in the heart of the world.

Since this view emphasizes the unique gifts and capacities of each member, it may lead to diversification in ministries. The sense of corporateness lies in the group itself and in the mutual relationships among the members. The sense of corporateness within the whole congregation, beyond the personal grouping of the local community, may suffer in this model unless a special effort is made to maintain relational bonds among the small groups within the same congregation. "Clusters" or "areas" are sometimes established within a congregation for this purpose. This third model tends to be taking on a special importance in many religious communities in recent years.

Every aspect of religious life could be analyzed in the light of these three cultural outlooks. Each of them has its unique richness, but I believe that the graced history of our present moment points in the general direction of the post-modern paradigm as the challenge of our age. It is a pattern that is only beginning to be realized and demands conscious choices of those who live it—choices that will be transformative personally and corporately.

Our ancestors in religious life grappled with similar tensions at each of the decisive moments in church history and succeeded in producing syntheses that channeled and evoked Christian vitality, dedication, and holiness. Or sometimes they failed, and their communities withered and died. Our challenge, amid the cultural conflicts of our age, is to collaborate in fashioning a way of life that will channel the best Christian generosity of our time.

CHAPTER 3

FACETS OF POVERTY

Each of the vows is uniquely challenging. But today, in a world torn by struggles between rich and poor, and in a church sensitive to social justice as an integral part of its gospel mission, the vow of poverty is particularly important and perplexing.

The vow of poverty is ultimately a spiritual stance, but we all know that poverty of spirit amid a life of luxury is an illusion and an occasion of mockery. We know that in itself poverty is not a good — rather an evil to combat — and we wonder if we are really helping poor people combat it. We are aware that consumerism and conspicuous consumption are key problems in modern society in all parts of the world. When we eavesdrop on conversations in public places, we are amazed at how much centers in gadgets, machines, comforts, and incomes. We wonder how we can work against these problems within ourselves and in our ministry to others.

It is my conviction — more an intuition than a reasoned conclusion — that renewal and vitality for religious depends much more than we usually suspect on the seriousness with which we take the vow of poverty. In poor environments people instinctively judge spiritual vitality by a willing and cheerful simplicity of life and by solidarity with the poor in their struggles for dignity, liberation, and justice. And, despite their inevitable resistance, rich and comfortable Christians are becoming increasingly sensitive to the global and local realities of the poor. They look to religious for a sense of compassion and a motivation to convert from what they increasingly recognize as an exploitative and wasteful lifestyle.

No religious figures have exerted a powerful appeal in our century if they were not marked by extraordinary sensitivity to the problems of poverty; Mother Teresa is the latest of a long line of figures including such visionaries as Charles de Foucauld, Mahatma Gandhi, Dorothy Day, Dom Helder Camara — and in their unique way, nearly all of our popes, particularly those since John XXIII. The mark of true religion in our century repeats in a new and particularly compelling way the criteria of the letter of James: "Pure and undefiled religion before God and the Father is this: to visit the fatherless and widows in their affliction. . . ."

THE ROOTS OF TODAY'S MENTALITY

Yet the feelings of most of us religious today are confused in the sphere of economic life. In the lifetimes of many of us, the Great Depression of the '30s and the Second World War — both times of great deprivation — were formative experiences which affected attitudes quite profoundly. These experiences taught us to scrimp and save, to value security — and to long for a time when we might sit back and enjoy greater abundance. Deprivation was imposed more than chosen, and we emerged looking upon our straitened circumstances as a bitter pill, counseling caution but promising a time of abundance after a long but temporary season of sacrifice.

It was only in the late '50s and '60s that we began to breathe more freely again. These were times of institutional expansion, accompanied by a considerable escalation in our lifestyle. Together with the general middle-class culture of the time, we began to enjoy higher standards in housing, food and drink, clothing, and the thousands of gadgets with which a consumer society, like a new Circe, lured us to visions of a better life.

At the same time, the new winds of religious thought encouraged us to update our asceticism and remove the Jansenistic overlay that had provided some of the legitimization and vocabulary of sacrifice in the preceding era. Much of this was undoubtedly good and long overdue. But perhaps in some cases we thought we were affirming the beauty and goodness of creation and leading the church resolutely into the modern world when, in fact, we were just letting the noonday devils of comfort and consumerism get a good grip upon us. As Father Arrupe, Superior General of the Jesuits, once said, *homo sapiens* in our time has increasingly become *homo consumens.* Religious have not been exempt from this consumeristic drift, whether they work in rich countries or in poor.

Sometime in the '70s we religious in the West began to become at least marginally aware of some new realities. Our comfortable lifestyle had been bought at a high human price.

Expanding global consciousness helped us to realize that our consumerism was closely linked to the suffering of the poor peoples of the world. We began to recognize that world resources were limited, and that we were often among those who were using them up at an alarming rate. We tried in little ways to adapt, and we started feeling vaguely guilty about such affluence as we possessed. Quite a few of us felt the urge to do something more (we weren't sure just what) for the poor. The response seemed clearer in the poorer countries than in those of Europe and North America, but even in the Third World the societal stance and impact of religious was often subject to question and critique. The complexities of the problem tended to immobilize us. What difference could our small efforts make toward the solution of a massive global crisis?

I have dwelt on these bits of history because I believe that they leave us with a rather complex set of attitudes regarding material goods. Many of us still feel the instincts for security, parsimony, and resistance to imposed deprivation that are the heritage of the '30s and '40s.

The liberating mentality of appreciation for the good things of life and creation and the habits of comfort and good taste which we learned in the '50s and '60s continue to attract us. Yet they seem somehow in contradiction to the new concern for poverty and justice which burst upon the church in the '70s. Our minds, hearts, and nervous systems are filled with a lot of unintegrated and confusing impulses.

No essay can disentangle the confusion. No one person has the answer. The following reflections are offered more as a stimulus to thought and prayer than anything else. If we approach the conundrums of vowed poverty with mutual respect, with understanding for each one's needs, and with an openness to the full gospel message, we can, over time, come to a common mind and a common witness that will speak to the vague but demanding stirrings of our time and enable us to stand more at one with those figures who have sparked the religious idealism and imagination of our day by their witness of poverty.

POVERTY AND SHARING OF GOODS

At its most elementary level, the poverty we vow as religious involves a sharing in common of whatever goods we possess. At least, the minimum in the observance of poverty involves being content with the goods we possess in common. We must challenge the tendency to amass private property, however it is manifested in different situations and different cultures.

Sharing in common does not necessarily give a striking witness of austerity, but it does bring us together. The loneliness and mutual indifference we sometimes deplore are often the product of too many exceptions to community of goods—too many personal possessions and conveniences that absorb our time and attention and draw us away from any felt need for one another. The need to share our goods, to compromise in our preferences, to be satisfied with the common supply—all this provides numerous opportunities for that support and challenge which are the essence of community life. The sharing of goods thus offers a basis for the sharing of interests, concerns, memories, aspirations, and prayer.

In the fifteenth century religious life hit its nadir when the monks and friars of the time deserted the common table in favor of food cooked to their personal taste by their private servants.

In the twentieth century the atmosphere of the religious house as a "comfortable second-class hotel for religiously minded persons" may represent the same kind of abuse.

The challenge to share does not stop at the gates of our religious communities. Our common goods are the wealth of the Church, and the way we use them is one of our most powerful opportunities for good or bad, evangelization or scandal. If we show a collective stinginess, hoarding in locked strongholds what we have only for ourselves and a few close and trusted friends, we naturally evoke hostility. If we constantly seek to share with many others as much as we can — despite headaches and frustrations, disappointments and seeming waste, despite possibilities of sometimes being abused and cheated — we give a powerful and unusual witness in today's individualistic and consumeristic culture. Sharing goods and facilities is, again, often the first step towards a much deeper sense of community with those around us.

SIMPLICITY

A somewhat more demanding level of poverty involves a consistent effort at de-escalating our consumeristic habits. Many of us have become too dependent on our creature comforts, as those who spend any time in a third-world country quickly discover: the body goes to pieces and peace of mind is shattered when accustomed comforts disappear.

Simplicity, even a touch of austerity, is among the expectations which today's people, especially the youth, place upon those who claim to be religious. People who make no pretense at simplicity themselves want to see it in us. Perhaps there is a widespread sense that consumeristic materialism is an evil — an addiction like smoking or alcoholism, which people would be rid of if they could, but which only a few have the courage to combat. At any rate, it is quite clear that nothing speaks more compellingly of holiness than a simple, undemanding, austere lifestyle; conversely, nothing arouses more disbelief and alienation than the aroma of luxury among the professionally religious.

Quite apart from their witness value, however, simplicity and austerity have a way of laying bare our relationship with God. Freed from the distractions and the illusory reassurance of our little comforts and luxuries, we stand before God a little more as we are — as human beings longing for God, needing God's mercy, never to be fulfilled or satisfied except in God. Too many material possessions lull us into forgetfulness of who made us and why we are here. The universal experience of all religions bears witness to that. A more austere life opens new or forgotten vistas of the knowledge of God.

It is important to realize that in today's world, viewed on a global scale, religious, with their high level of education and international networks of support, form part of a privileged minority. They can hardly live like the destitute — without security, without minimum necessities, often without work. The spiritual benefits of such destitution — for oneself and for others — are highly doubtful. Yet there are surely some creeping attachments in the lives of each of us that could stand pruning.

Such an examination of conscience will be valuable in the measure that we humbly look to ourselves and avoid pointing fingers at others. Many of our gingerly attempts to approach this delicate point are stymied by brick throwing. We spend much of our time threatening one another, berating motes in our brothers' and sisters' eyes and studiously avoiding the planks in our own.

Simplicity of life is never easy for an individual or for a community. Each age group, each type of personality, each human culture has its strong points and weaknesses in this domain. What a powerful witness we would give if we could all share one another's strengths! We must move beyond that kind of accusatory stance which hardens us to one another and immobilizes personal and community good will. If we aim at a more "sparing and sharing" lifestyle, we will surely discover some changes we can make and, in the process, come closer to God, to one another, and to the people of God around us.

SPIRIT OF DETACHMENT

Vowed poverty without material simplicity is rightly regarded with suspicion. Yet it remains true that the faithful observance of the vow cannot be measured in purely economic terms. The deepest meaning of our vow of poverty challenges us to a detachment in spiritual domains as well as material ones.

In a subtle way we "possess" (or are "possessed by") roles, habits, jobs, people, and places. It is easy for us to base our feelings of security and self-worth on particular jobs to which we tenaciously cling, on routines and practices we unnecessarily canonize, on institutions which we dominate, or on particular places we feel we cannot leave.

Such attachments are usually the result of great dedication and commitment. But the commitment ossifies a bit, grows cold and sterile, because it is too little open to change. What began as a good becomes harmful—harmful to us personally and to our corporate mission—when it prevents us from hearing new calls and experiencing new challenges, from turning over the good we have cultivated to new, likewise dedicated, hands. Our excessive attachment to one good sometimes does not leave us free for many other goods.

Such attachments to nonmaterial things are difficult to identify and handle. Others can usually spot them in us before we detect them ourselves. The spirit of poverty challenges us to let go and promises a new freedom when we do so.

SOLIDARITY WITH THE POOR

One of the greatest challenges to our apostolic creativity today is that of finding ways to serve the poor and stand with them in their struggles.

It seems pretty clear that we cannot avoid the challenge on the plea that "we can't do everything" or it is "not our apostolate." The church of today is so obviously called to a refocussing of energies on the poor that it is useless to claim to be one with that church and shrug off the call.

One way is to undertake new works and ministries. This effort seems particularly important in mobilizing some of the most creative energies of religious today. New works in solidarity with the poor will require time and an experience of trial and error for most communities.

But another major challenge is to reorient our work in present apostolates. Justice for the poor — that justice which is an integral part of the gospel message (as the Synod of 1971 put it) — should be a preoccupation everywhere. When we work among the comfortable and well off, the challenge is to motivate them to help, to broaden their thinking, and to stimulate their good will. Programs need to involve well-off participants in actually experiencing the problems of the poor and marginalized.

In the West, and sometimes even in very poor countries, contemporary society insulates us too much from one another. It is easy for many of us and our students, parishioners, and fellow-workers to go through life with very minimal contacts with the really poor. Experience — a little rubbing of shoulders and looking one another in the face — is probably the necessary first step. We may not solve anyone's problems, but at least we may learn to stand a little closer and to feel more deeply the pains of those who are not so privileged as we. The result might be at least as beneficial for us and our well-to-do associates as it is for the poor. Time spent in the so-called mission areas generally opens eyes and especially hearts to these problems. But the same will happen if we just try to gain some more experience of the poor in any environment. They are everywhere, only a little better hidden in some places.

Perhaps the most important aim at this stage should be solidarity. Material destitution is an evil; we don't want to idealize it, but overcome it as effectively as possible. We cannot pretend to be exactly like the poor. But we can get to know them and share their concerns and burdens more fully. Our education and our influence can help give voice and understanding to their difficult lot. Their unique experience of God and divine providence may be a deep spiritual enrichment for us. Some of the richest forms of worship and devotion stem from the poor. They have much to give us if we get to know them. That is the meaning of solidarity — we stand together as Mary stood with John beneath the cross, and all experience a new source of power.

This essay is quite incomplete. It is very much a series of jottings in a pilgrim's notebook. It will doubtless raise more questions than it answers. We are living in a time when our vow of poverty places all of us very deeply in question. But the questioning is God's gentle prodding—not an effort to uproot and destroy, but rather to plant and build.

CHAPTER 4

THE HOLE IN THE HEART

A Life of Chastity

Not many contemporary opinion-leaders propound celibate chastity as an approved lifestyle. Yet, in fact, many people live this lifestyle, more or less consistently, for motives of career, humanitarian service, art, care for parents or for the sick, or even for fear or selfishness. The celibate chastity underlying our religious commitment is that which is undertaken "for the sake of the kingdom."

Any kind of chastity leaves us with intensified longings and drives. As religious we aim to channel these into deepened self-knowledge and integration, into the love of the Lord, and into the service of God's people in ministry.

THE HOLE IN THE HEART

The drive toward relationships with other people, expressed in physical and spiritual ways, is fundamental in human life. In many ways our conscious relatedness is that which is most human about us. By promising to abstain from genital relationships and from the foundation of a human family, we are touching what is most human about us. We should certainly expect some intense feelings and challenges if we embrace this kind of chastity. We should also expect some painful times. There is no doubt that this kind of abstinence leaves a gaping hole or chasm in the heart of the human person.

Such abstinence can only be a holy and healthy choice if we honestly face that "hole" and seek to focus our energy and our longing on the enhancing and humanizing of life, on the Lord in the life of prayer, and on generous service to others.

The idea, as expressed by Matthew Fox, is to be, in imitation of Jesus, a "truly emptied person ... so vulnerable to beauty and truth, to justice and compassion, that he or she becomes a truly hollow and hallowed channel for divine grace" (Matthew Fox, O.P., *Original Blessing* [Santa Fe: Bear and Co., 1983], p. 172).

We probably need to be much clearer and more frank than we have been in the past about this hollowness, this gaping hole the practice of the vow of chastity leaves in our hearts. Celibate chastity surely does not reduce our natural longings and our drives. In fact, I believe it is meant to intensify them. By denying them satisfaction at the most obvious level, we are propelled into an ongoing conscious channeling of the energy that flows from these longings and drives. The whole problem of celibate chastity concerns the focus of that energy.

One of the harder parts in the vow of chastity lies in the lack of permanency in our relationships. Because we are not entering into a covenant-bond such as marriage with any other human person, the intimate human relationships that we experience tend to come and go with distressing frequency. Friends, students, and parishioners pass in and out of our lives, sometimes attaining great depth of intimacy, but we cannot really count on any of them being present to us permanently.

It is not easy to go through life without ever being the primary "gleam in someone else's eyes," or missing the constant companionship and responsibility of family life. Many other kinds of relationships and responsibilities can come our way through the freedom that the vow of chastity gives us. But we should expect that our longing and our needs for human relatedness will be, at least at certain times, particularly intense. If the vow means anything, it means that we keep that hole open, ready to be filled in the Lord's way by our conscious focus on him and on the many different people he sends into our lives.

The chasm, the empty spot in our heart, is at the core of our commitment to celibate chastity for the sake of the kingdom. We stand before God with that empty place in our hearts and live in hope and trust that God will use it and fill it.

CHASTITY AND RELIGIOUS EXPERIENCE

Religious experience is the key to the meaningful living of chastity. God is the permanent relationship in our lives, and no human being ultimately is. This fact is true for everyone, but religious life sharpens the experience of our fundamental solitude, makes it more blunt and obvious. This kind of life is appropriately undertaken only in the faith that God will make our heart a source of life-giving, unselfish, universal love. The religious search for an undivided heart that reaches out to God and others is the fundamental motivation for our vow of chastity.

The religious who does not live an intense love for God will find the hole in the heart pretty meaningless and will probably start looking for other compensations—career, work, comforts, possessions, relationships that skate on the edge of the promise of chastity.

There is no formula for dealing with the hole in the heart. No level of maturity, no techniques of human and religious development, no combination of ministry and friendship will insulate us from the pain and the challenge of celibacy for the sake of the kingdom.

The lessons of nearly a century of psychoanalysis seem to be teaching us that life's greatest and most important problems do not admit of solution. All we can do is outgrow them, see them as "mystery" and "opportunity" more than as "problem." As richer and broader interests lighten our horizon, some of our problems lose their oppressive urgency. A new life-energy, a new level of consciousness fills our hearts and eases some of our pains.

The hole in the heart left by our abstinence from permanent genital relationships cannot be adequately filled, but the urgency of the pain and its place in our over-all life can fade as we find our energy liberated for broader and larger concerns. Celibacy will not be much helped by introspective reflection on celibacy. It will only be an energizing way of life when our hearts are reaching out for other goods. That is why celibacy must be "for the sake of the kingdom."

WHERE WE HAVE COME FROM

Despite our idealistic motivations, most of us are pretty aware that our personal and collective histories of living celibate chastity are full of flaws. Together with the culture around us — perhaps more intensely than much of that culture — we have experienced a great deal of repression and negativity in regard to sexuality and the whole human drive for relatedness.

For many years the norm in religious life was not to talk about such things. We were encouraged to act as if we had no sexual drives. The less said, the less thought about this dimension of our life, the better. "Rules of precaution and reserve" — surely necessary — were exaggerated and understood in a way that blocked energy instead of releasing and channeling it. When "temptations" came, we were urged to react by flight or by some kind of psychological violence.

The result was usually compensation. People sometimes experience religious as rather "asexual," withdrawn from any kinds of relationships perhaps out of fear, but plowing all their life-energies into careers, institutions, or other kinds of material or spiritual satisfactions which are, at best, not quite integrally human. Another result has sometimes been a certain indifference, a lack of understanding and compassion for others ("if I have to repress my problematic drives, why can't they?"). We need to reflect more honestly and openly on the relational and the sexual dimensions of our lives and to deal much more honestly and openly with them.

In general, our approach to our own sexuality might be grouped into three classes.

Some deal with sexual drives mostly by repression. These people are usually seen as being in some way emotionally immature. They often compensate for their lack of emotional development by inappropriate, distorted, sometimes neurotic actions, and by a whole gamut of misdirected emotional energies (compensations). These dynamics of repression were characteristic of society in general around the beginning of this century.

Others have an emotional life characterized by what Freud termed "the return of the repressed." For these people the repression of sexual drives becomes subconsciously intolerable, and they find themselves compelled to express these drives by abnormal or typically adolescent behavior. These people, unlike the first group, are usually rather aware of their sexual emotions, but this awareness is for them mainly a problem, and they feel helpless, ashamed, guilty, but unable to "contain themselves" (i.e., to revert wholly to the previous stage of repression). They have a compulsive drive to express their sexual emotions in some kind of overt activity. Such compulsive sexual hedonism, self-centered rather than other-centered, seems characteristic of our own time. Books, films, and TV shows are supersaturated with selfish eroticism, perhaps in a misguided attempt to break through the immature, guilt-laden heritage of a repressive society.

Some have well-integrated sexual drives. These people are at peace with accepting their sexual feelings without shame or guilt, but without being compelled to act out these emotions in ways contrary to their commitments. They are able to have strong and positive relationships with others—relationships marked by much warmth and affectivity—without exclusivity, possessiveness, jealousy, and patterns of domination. The vow of chastity is prophetic if it educates our hearts to such well-integrated relationships.

The preceding three categories arc classifications that help us think about concrete situations. No one fits perfectly and exclusively into any one category. Even the "best integrated" find celibate love a source of frequent struggle, and even the "most repressed" experience and give some genuine, well-developed, and appropriate love-responses.

A DEVELOPMENTAL APPROACH

If there is one conviction I would like to share above all others, it is that celibate chastity is something that we grow in. Chastity involves a life-long growth process. We take such a process for granted when we speak of poverty and obedience, or other aspects of religious life like prayer, community life or apostolic dedication. We take it for granted that there should be a positive growth in our lives toward the integration of all these values. But somehow we have tended to think that chastity is an either/or situation. Either you are chaste or you are not. There are no degrees and no possibility of growth in this matter.

On the contrary, I believe that no consciousness of growth and ongoing challenge in the matter of chastity is a sign of stagnation. It is true that genital activity is something which we either do or do not do. But beyond that, the whole dealing with the "hole in the heart," the growth in our motivation and channeling of energy to the Lord and to our fellow religious and to the people we serve, the deeper integration of all dimensions of being human in our own life, the channeling of our drive for sexuality and relatedness into a genuine and healthy gift of self to other people — all of this admits of, and even requires, constant growth.

I fear that sometimes — traumatized by our fear of relationships and deeply repressing much of the energy for love that is within us — we may stop growing altogether. Sin is essentially a self-centered lack of love. It is as serious a sin — although of a different type — to constrict the gift of ourselves to other people and to stifle love, as it is to have genital relations without love. Self-centeredness is the fundamental sin. Love is the key focus of holiness.

Even in the area of genital abstinence, there can certainly be a growth in consistency and fidelity. Failings against such abstinence are particularly troublesome because of their implications for ourselves and for other people. But God can even sometimes use these kinds of failings as a springboard to deepening and growth. We should certainly not be surprised that we are sometimes tempted in this way. God is very demanding, but also very forgiving, sensitive to our humanity, very much a saving God who brings the best even out of our mistakes and lapses. We should not condone these, but we should not lose hope or be unforgiving, to ourselves or others, if they occur.

CHASTITY AND BODILINESS

In an effort to promote chastity, some of our religious formation in the past tended toward angelism. We did not always recognize and give appropriate place to the needs of our bodies. Modesty is a virtue, but it is excessive if it means prudishness or dislike for the body.

Some of the malformation of our past has left many of us feeling somehow not very comfortable in our own skins. We are still afflicted by the imprint of a dualistic education, which made us feel that the body was evil and only the spirit was good.

When we relate to one another, we always do so through the body. It is important for us to come back into contact with natural body expression. There is sometimes a tension in our ways of relating to one another and to the people we meet and know and serve. Feeling and touching is a natural part of human relating. Every expression of it is not part of foreplay leading to genital activity!

And yet, I am afraid that, out of an exaggerated fear, we have often shrunk from even the most innocent forms of physical contact—a pat on the back, a hug, a warm handshake. Cultures differ greatly in the significance they attach to such gestures. But in every culture the body plays a key role in expressing warmth and affection.

When the repression of bodily expression becomes intolerable, we are tempted to plunge into compulsive sensuality and eroticism. "Precaution" and "reserve," poorly understood, thus end up in compulsive hedonism. That is pretty much the story of general culture and communications media in the twentieth century. The best help to chastity is not inhibition, but an ongoing, respectful care for our physical and psychic needs, so that our bodies become part of a whole person perceived as holy, as a channel of grace and gracefulness.

A sane and balanced interest in our own bodies, a savoring of the beauty of the human form in all its varieties, from the beauty of youth to the beauty of age—all of this is part of the thankfulness for creation and the integral holiness to which we are called. Such attitudes support our living of the vow rather than undermine it. They are genuine helps to chastity. The vow of chastity is not a vow of ignoring the body. It is rather a vow of channeling the creative and expressive energies of our bodies into the life of holiness.

We need to accept and love our human bodies. This acceptance and love includes our sexuality and our hard-to-integrate sexual desires. They are God's gift to us. It would be good for us to reflect on whether or not there is excessive fear or excessive prudishness about the bodily dimension of our lives. Rather than repressing any attention given to human bodies—our own or others—we should learn to be thankful and joyous for the beauty of God's creation mediated to us through human corporeality. The result will probably be greater relaxation and greater attention to what our body tells us about the whole of our body-spirit nature.

PERSONAL RELATIONSHIPS

Human intimacy must be a key focus of our living of chastity. To be intimate is to let another into our lives in such a way that his or her presence becomes a part of our own self-image and self-worth. Intimacy involves, therefore, a certain "dying to self" and a "loving our neighbor as ourselves." Because intimacy is so costly, we have a great variety of ways of protecting and defending ourselves from it. Yet some intimate relationships are necessary for a fully integrated and fully generous life.

In religious life intimacy is somewhat more difficult than it is in lay life. The more intimate we are with a person, the harder it is to leave that person. Yet celibate love, in its universality, implies the willingness to let many others into our lives, and also the willingness to let them out. Since the process of letting go is very painful, we may tend to develop strong resistance to intimacy of any kind.

Moreover, intimacy by its nature tends to physical expression, and any development of intimacy within a celibate religious commitment will often create a tension concerning physical expression which will also be painful and difficult to deal with. The "easy way out" is to avoid intimacy rather than develop the attitudes necessary for celibate intimacy. But avoidance is possible only by repression and compensation. We tend to withdraw from intimacy and invest our self-worth somewhere other than in persons — in work, in roles, functions, accomplishments, comforts, and the like.

It is striking, nonetheless, how intimacy characterized so many of the relationships of Jesus (the Twelve, Martha and Mary) and how intimacy with others (including intimacy with the Lord himself) is so powerful a factor in the lives of the saints. The ideal is the willingness to make the investment of intimacy not only in "worthy" people, but also in the "little ones": the poor, the sick, children, the handicapped. At this point, the living of intimacy within a celibate religious commitment touches very closely on the living of a commitment of solidarity with the poor, the suffering, the marginal.

The celibate religious can attain genuine intimacy. But awareness of sexuality must be integrated into the desire — equally an emotional drive — to live out Christ's universal, healing, redemptive, and compassionate love.

THE MASCULINE AND THE FEMININE

The holy and healthy living of celibate chastity also gives rise to reflection on "masculine" and "feminine" aspects within ourselves. We usually think of the "masculine" as the side of ourselves that expresses energy, dominance, courage, reason — the conscious and active, controlling side. The "feminine" involves sensitivity, depth of feeling, receptivity, the ability to be passive and accept, affirm others. All people have both dimensions present in some way within themselves. The cultural and possibly biological predominance of the "masculine" qualities in males and the "feminine" qualities in females is a difference of emphasis or of ratio between these sets of qualities. It is not a question of either/or — males having only "masculine" qualities, females only "feminine" ones.

I believe that celibacy impels us toward a more conscious development of both the masculine dimensions and the feminine ones in our personality. It can lead, to those who follow it faithfully through much pain and struggle, to a depth of integration and a kind of holiness which spontaneously minister to others.

Full human development and integrated holiness require the development of both dimensions. A covenant relationship like marriage between two persons of opposite sexes tends to develop this kind of wholeness in the couple. Through interaction with the woman, the man becomes more aware of feelings, more receptive and gentle; through interaction with the man, the woman becomes more assertive, dominant. The interaction of the couple over a series of years creates real growth — or has the potential to do so — in both as individuals, but the main focus of their integrated whole humanity comes in their action as couple.

In celibacy, such integration, if it is to happen, must take place more in the individual self. Integration requires consciousness of the development of both sides of the human person. It intensifies feelings, which cannot be acted out or projected so easily onto the other member of a couple. It sometimes leaves us feeling like a bubbling pot, confused and pulled by contradictory emotions. If we remain faithful to the development of these feelings, rather than trying to deny or repress them, in the long run the living of celibacy evokes within each of us a more conscious and personalized development of both masculine and feminine characteristics.

Many religious women are strong, courageous, and powerful leaders. They do not lack "femininity," but they display a human integration which is perhaps some sign of the grace of celibate chastity I am trying to describe here. Similarly, many religious men are genuinely warm, gentle, receptive. Such persons are not unenergetic or passive; they have attained a striking level of integration. Most of us do not feel very whole or integrated in the different dimensions of our personality. But I believe that one of the long-range effects of celibate chastity can be such an integrated holiness as an individual.

Of course, celibate persons do not and should not live in isolation from the opposite sex. There is perhaps nothing more characteristic of the change of mentality in spirituality in recent years than the greater openness to such relationships. Past prohibitions and prudish cautions were very harmful. We need to learn to relate to one another not as objects of erotic self-satisfaction, but as partners in ministry and in human experiences. Our relationships will then lead to depth and richness, to new levels of holiness.

DANGERS AND WEAKNESSES

The attitudes I am speaking of here have their dangers. Our vow is a promise of abstinence. In the short run greater attention to our bodies, to warm relationships with others, to ongoing growth, provides challenges and tensions which make genital abstinence difficult. But in the long run I believe that it is only such attitudes which allow us to attain the kind of human and religious development which will be a blessing and a mediation of salvation to those around us.

In the process of this kind of development we will certainly have "temptations" to deal with. There is no way to avoid the wisdom of the tradition on this point. Sometimes the creative and expressive energy of sexuality will come out in autoeroticism. Sometimes it will come out in powerful attractions for the other sex. Sometimes, in many if not most religious, it will come out in the form of erotic attractions for the same sex. As long as we are sincerely struggling for the integration of our feelings in accord with our promise of abstinence we should not be too overwhelmed or upset by powerful erotic longings. It would not be human to go through life without a good measure of them.

Our past formation (not only religious formation but the formation given by society in general) has left us with the feeling that attractions for the other sex were natural (if a sad and evil temptation for celibates), but that any other kinds of erotic longings were pathological. I do not believe that this is true. Whether it is a matter of stages of growth or of different kinds of sexual orientation, it is certainly true that attractions for our own bodies as something erotic and for others of both sexes are fairly normal, if not universal, parts of human experience.

God made bodies beautiful, and we should not be surprised that we feel some of our creative energy reaching out toward them, without a rigorous distinction of only attractions for women among men and only attractions for men among women. There is probably a spectrum of such feeling-orientations. Many find almost all their love-energy galvanized by the other sex and rarely experience any other kinds of attractions. Some, for whatever reason, find themselves much more readily attracted by their own sex. Some find themselves pretty much in the middle.

An attraction is neither good nor evil. In particular, I do not believe that the situation of living in a single-sex religious community today either enhances or deflects in a very significant way these innate longings which are unique to each individual. I do not believe that there is anything shameful, pathological, or incompatible with religious life about an attraction that includes homosexual feelings.

Again, our promise of celibacy is a promise of genital abstinence. It is a promise to leave the chasm in our hearts empty of the kinds of immediate satisfaction which flow from genital relationships. Our vow is most importantly a promise to channel the creative drives and energies deriving from our love relationships into holiness and ministry. As long as we are focussing in that way, we need not be excessively preoccupied with the particular forms our erotic longings may take.

We need to accept our particular experiences of sexual attraction, not mainly as troubles, but above all as God's way of summoning us to grow in love. Only such an acceptance will remove from us the fears, twisted projections, and unrealistic fantasies which come from excessive repression. Because the process of development is so delicate and so challenging, spiritual direction is essential in this domain. We cannot achieve integral holiness alone, but we will become richer and deeper as religious, more genuine as human persons, more whole in our living of abstinence, more giving of ourselves, and richer in the outpourings from the chasm of our hearts, if we allow such developments to take place in our lives.

Sexuality has been a key focus of feelings and thought since the dawn of the human race. Celibacy and its meaning have been a religious preoccupation, in Christianity and beyond, for many centuries. There is nothing all that new in what I have written here.

What might be new today is our heightened awareness of the extent and depth of sexual feeling in influencing our lives. For many of us, this heightened awareness raises many questions and stirs up some troublesome emotions. I hope that these thoughts may be of some help. Their main thrust is to encourage us not to look at our sexual selves as a problem but rather as a mystery, so that we can plunge more deeply and genuinely into love for God's creation.

At the end of creation, God looked at everything and "saw that it was good." Our hope should be that we may learn to regard all God's physical creation, including ourselves and our physical sexuality, as part of a loving goodness.

CHAPTER 5

A LISTENING HEART

The Vow of Obedience

In a famous passage of the First Book of Kings (3:9), Solomon prays for a "listening heart" to discern wisely between good and evil. Many of us find inspiration in this passage for the sense of intuitive attentiveness we desire in opening our lives to God.

Religious on the whole are characterized by a desire to be faithful to the vow of obedience, to follow the will of God. The problems and challenges we meet regarding this vow are more related to different assumptions and insights than to any lack of desire for fidelity.

Many feel that they are in something of a muddle about authority and obedience. Some would like to rediscover the unquestioning kind of clarity which religious perhaps used to feel about such matters, back before Vatican II.

But we should not expect to clear up the muddle once and for all.

We should not expect that the mutual exercise of authority and obedience will become easy. We should not expect that it will all be "cut and dried," with no room for a margin of error, no call for a leap and wager of faith, which knows that it might possibly be wrong.

Questions of authority and obedience are above all questions of faith—the kind of faith that trusts and has confidence, but that lives very much in darkness and obscurity. Authority and obedience are not meant to clear up the darkness and obscurity, so that we can go ahead with life in some kind of triumphant and possibly smug assurance that we are doing God's will. Authority and obedience are part of the mystery which is the object of belief, not a way of clearing up the mystery of our lives.

Authority and obedience exist precisely because religious are presumed to be people in a seeking posture, looking, scanning the signs of the times, trying to discover in the muddle of the world some clues for the "will of God." Once we stop seeking, once we feel secure that we have found exactly what God wants for us and can serenely proceed to do it without any kind of wondering—then we can be pretty sure that we have cut down the mystery to our own size, and that we are cutting out some of God's action in our lives.

A SPECTRUM OF CONCEPTS AND THEOLOGIES

Religious today have differing expectations concerning authority and obedience. When questions of obedience and authority come up, there is often a strong and deep division. Some bitterly complain that the role of authority and obedience is usually exaggerated or at least falsely presented. These point to the danger of seeing the superior as a dictator, fostering the "cult of personality" of religious leaders, and supporting the many excesses and abuses of religious authority ingrained in our consciousness. For these it is hardly possible to speak of the vow of obedience without being hopelessly authoritarian, lost in a hierarchical consciousness that might have been acceptable sometime in the Age of Absolutism, but that is unthinkable at present.

According to others, authority and obedience are disappearing (or, indeed, have long since disappeared) in religious congregations. We no longer have a strong leadership that knows how to command, or subjects who know how to obey. We are drifting aimlessly, and all the talk about leadership only confirms the general wishy-washiness of the times. These people plead for a much more exigent authority, one that is not afraid to command, to correct abuses, and, in general, to give the boot to persons and things that should not be. Of course, very few complain that authority has been too easy on them personally (on the contrary), but it is thought to be obviously much too lenient with nearly everyone else!

Such reactions represent only a small percentage of religious. Yet these reactions demonstrate a considerable polarization and difference of opinion about authority and obedience. The reactions cannot neatly be divided into conservative and liberal, or old and young. Some people usually labelled young and liberal plead for a stronger, more exigent authority that would give a clearer and more unified direction; some people usually labelled old and conservative evidently feel pushed and sat upon by the modern exercise of authority, forced into molds of decision-making with which they are profoundly uncomfortable.

A few points are clear as we try to analyze this difference of opinion — one which seems to be common to all religious societies today:

- There is a theology which places great emphasis on the mediation of the will of God for me through the superior; this theology is impatient with emphasis on any other mediations (like the will of God in daily events, in cultural changes, in the opinions and suggestions of one's fellow religious, etc.); this theology tends to correlate with a "vertical" kind of spirituality, which stresses a hierarchical and direct relationship between God and me.
- There is another theology which places great emphasis on community and participatory decision-making as privileged places for the mediation of the will of God; the role of the superior is sometimes a problem in this theology; much greater play is given to individual lights and inspirations in this theology, and there is a great fear of "quenching the Spirit" by too many interventions from above; this theology often correlates with a "horizontal" kind of spirituality, which stresses

the meeting of God in people, activities, events, and my immediate environment.

- Most people accept elements of both theologies and spiritualities, but are confused about how to integrate them.
- The stances taken are culturally influenced.

North Americans are proud of their democratic, participative traditions, and tend to transfer attitudes customary in
political life into the realm of religious authority and obedience. This is their contribution, which may be unique and
especially stimulating to religious life today. It may also
obscure some other elements necessary in the search for the
will of God. Freedom, due process, participatory decision-
making, and majority rule do not exhaust our routes to the
will of God.

Latin cultures tend to be more paternalistic, to look for a
strong leadership, but also to react more strongly to authori-
tarianism.

South Asian culture emphasizes an almost absolute claim
of one's spiritual guide, but this claim must first be earned
through the experience of a powerful personal relationship.
South Asians have great external respect but also considerable
inner cynicism and distrust toward purely institutional authority. They prefer personal negotiation to structured channels.

Each of the world's many cultures has something to give and
something to learn from the others when it comes to searching
for God's will. Each provides room for the freedom of the
children of God and a strong independence, born of a deep
sense of vocation; each also provides room for unity of direction and the mysterious sense of total commitment to a life-
project that transcends the career of any one individual.

When we try to find clarity about the will of God, we need
to examine our own instinctive conceptions a bit and see what
we can learn from that which is foreign to us. The Latin heritage of leadership by a "paterfamilias" opens up some rich
ways to God; the same is true of North American democracy,
the Asian concept of the guru, and the African concept of
authority and loyalty in the extended family.

HOW CAN WE UNDERSTAND AUTHORITY?

We often find ourselves defining a good sermon as "one that goes right over my own head and hits the person behind me smack between the eyes."

Perhaps many of us react this way especially to any talk about "authority." Authority, in our minds, instinctively, is something that other people exercise over us. It is a kind of domination, often not too intelligent, to which we are, regrettably, subject.

So the first point in our reflection on authority should be the recognition that every individual religious is a person of considerable authority. Religious exert influence and leadership and dominance in a unique way over many people. Many are "authorities" in classrooms, schools, parishes, pastoral teams, and within their local communities. But all are authoritative and influential in the broadest sense of the word. Religious belong to an educated elite, even those with the weakest training. They possess influence and authority, evoke respect and sometimes imitation because of their identification with the largest religious organization in the whole world. They can show up in quite a few places and command a bed and a little hospitality. It may be unsettling but true: most of the inhabitants of our planet have less authority, less influence, than does the most simple and obscure religious.

With this fact in mind, it becomes especially important for us to reflect on Jesus' teaching about authority as service. Jesus was a person of great authority, but he came "to serve and not to be served," and he taught his disciples that their authority should contrast radically with the "princes of this world" who "know how to make their authority felt." This "worldly" authority consists in the ability to impose one's will on others. Such authority is continued today by all those dictators and bosses and teachers and others who manage to pull off power-plays in the service of their own convenience, but also by those more suave, polished, and "hidden persuaders" who manage to plead and manipulate people to attain desired ends. Most of us religious, for good or evil, know something about this kind of manipulation, too — not only because we have often been manipulated, but also because we usually have some skill at manipulating others to get our will done.

That is not the kind of authority that characterized the kingdom of Jesus: "Let the one who is greatest among you be the servant of all."

The secret of the authority of Jesus was his ability to respond to the real aspirations, hopes, desires, and needs of others. He allowed them to use his power to work their wills — their deepest, most authentic good wills for healing, for empowering, for liberating. For him authority was service and it was empowerment. He asked us to be in the midst of the world as "one who serves."

Serve whom or what? Serve people in the attainment of their deepest aspirations, the aspirations that are at the core of their being as they have been created and called by God, aspirations which are often encrusted over by distortions, substitutes, false wants and needs.

It takes a great deal of discernment to know how to serve in this way. The use of the authority each of us has is the prime object of all our discernments. We all have great power to author life — or to stifle it. Discernment is first of all our effort to distinguish what will really be life-giving in the exercise of the personal authority we all have. Obedience is a listening process that empowers us to use our authority in a way that seems to be in tune with the will of God here and now.

AUTHORITY IN RELIGIOUS SOCIETIES

In a religious congregation, all the members have come together because, clearly or obscurely, they are seeking to discover the will of God and fulfill it. They come together in a particular religious congregation because, again clearly or obscurely, they experience God's call to participate in the common vocation, follow a common spiritual tradition, fulfill the common end, share the particular common charism.

It is the will of God at work in the initial discernment process that gives rise to the religious congregation, that also gives rise to some kind of institutionalized authority. The purpose of such authority is fidelity to the charism: to keep the congregation together and focussed in pursuing its aims, its fundamental vocation.

So it is that all authentic authority in a religious congregation comes from God. Unless the congregation itself, with its specific vocation and charism, comes from God, there is no genuine vocation and no genuine authority.

But we can also say that the authority arises in a way from the members. Religious are called to share in the common charism. In this common pursuit, they inevitably feel the need for guidance, direction, authoritative decision-making, above all to maintain unity and channel creativity, to serve, empower, and evoke life. We can trace the rise of such institutionalized authority in the history of the opening years of many religious movements and institutes. Most began as loose associations of companions, all thinking of themselves more or less as equals; little by little they delegate the authority intimately linked to their common charism to specific leaders or leadership groups who seem apt to exercise spiritual power and influence. So it is that authority comes at the same time from God and from the members. So it is, incidentally, that the experience of religious orders is at the origins of our Western traditions of democratic government, election, representativity, and the like.

This whole process, including its final point—the institutionalization of authority in a religious society by the creation of certain posts of governance—seems entirely justifiable, natural, and inevitable given our human condition. Institutionalized authority is an important factor in our lives. We should not exaggerate it or create a cult about it, but we should not think we can avoid it, either. Since it is natural and inevitable, it must be part of God's plan for us. Somewhere or other, it needs to be defined, delimited, and clearly specified, and we should not apologize for doing so, even though the end result may be a little on the legalistic side. It is important to know who has the authority to do what—where that authority begins and where it ends.

THE EXERCISE OF AUTHORITY

What has changed in the Catholic church since Vatican II has been less the existence, definition, rights, and limits of such authority, than the spirit in which it is exercised.

Formerly, such authority tended to be exercised in a rather monarchical way. There was something of the savor of the "princes of this world" sometimes about such exercise of authority. There could, indeed, be a "cult of personality." People suffered when authority imposed and stifled instead of serving and empowering.

Of course, abuses in the exercise of authority are not limited to the Catholic church, and they did not end with Vatican II. They are part of the temptation of sinful humanity. We all have authority, and we all tend to abuse it. Those entrusted with leadership in religious communities — superiors, gurus, or whatever — are not immune from these temptations.

But Vatican II called for an exercise of religious institutionalized authority in a way that was deeply influenced both by the gospel teaching of Jesus on service and empowerment and authoring life, and also by the democratic, participative modes of leadership that have become the ideal of some contemporary societies.

There are many ways of describing this relatively new spirit and mode of exercising religious authority. Much of this spirit can be summarized in four concepts: responsibility, participation, subsidiarity, and accountability.

The sense of responsibility requires each member to accept and carry out decisions and policies determined by the bearers and processes of authority that each community has recognized in its search for the will of God.

Participation consists in the active collaboration of all members, as much as possible, in planning, making, executing, and evaluating decisions. The use of communal discernment is a helpful means to attain full participation.

The principle of subsidiarity guides the appropriate authority to place decision-making at the level that is most competent and closest to those whom the decision will affect. It also obliges this authority to provide necessary support to those making the decision.

The principle of accountability obliges each member to keep competent authorities informed about the way in which he or she seeks to fulfil corporate goals. Those in authority have the duty of responding with constructive evaluation. This principle requires dispositions of openness and mutual responsibility.

This is a Western style of exercising leadership, no doubt, but it also corresponds to the growing search everywhere in our time for a personalized approach to finding the will of God. It allows many factors to make their proper contribution: common aims; congregational structures; interactions among members united in the same vocation; designated bearers of authority and trusted spiritual guides; and finally, in a unique way, each individual religious.

Each religious is called to make an active use of structures which facilitate the exercise of leadership, such as community meetings, discussions, and prayer. To refuse these responsibilities is not merely an absence of participation but a negative influence.

HOW CAN WE UNDERSTAND OBEDIENCE

Just as the word "authority" comes from a root (*augeo*) with overtones about life-giving and life-enhancing, so "obedience" comes from familiar Latin roots (*ob* + *audio*) that have to do with "listening." The desire for a "listening heart," a discerning fidelity to God, is at the core of our vow of obedience. In the Indian spiritual tradition, a similar quality is named *viveka*, the sensitive consciousness of divine reality within and about us.

To obey is to listen with this sensitive consciousness, carefully and faithfully, to the many varied voices and influences and authorities of all kinds that tell us something about the will of God.

To obey is to be patient enough to remain faithful to the

ongoing discernment of God's word here and now. Perhaps today we are most often disobedient because we are impatient, because we look for shortcuts, comfortable, tranquilizing ones, that allow us to have the satisfaction that we are doing "the will of God" without going through too much pain of listening and trying to understand, without the gradual cultivation of a discerning consciousness. This may happen because we are so attached to our own will that we never question it, or because we are overeager for a feeling of security.

Some parts of obedience are common to every religious person and have nothing specific to do with religious congregations; for example, the part of obedience that involves a discerning attentiveness to the world around us—to its strengths and weaknesses, its grace and sin, its hopes and aspirations, its fears and failures.

Another part of obedience valid for all is listening to the personal inspirations God offers uniquely to each individual. There is much room for self-deception here. Maybe too many people think they have too many strictly personal "inspirations of the Spirit." But genuine inspirations do come from time to time; they have surely been stifled in the past, and we need to listen to them carefully—and seek wise guidance in discerning what is genuine and what illusory.

We know much of what is God's will for us here and now when we have engaged in this obedience which is common to all those "who seek God with a sincere heart."

As religious we commit ourselves to a concrete congregation because we believe that we are called to participate in a special way in its grace and charism: in its particular aim and mission, and the specific scope of its vocation. Because of this conviction, which is at the source of every authentic religious vocation, we give a privileged place to certain additional voices in seeking to discover God's will.

We give a privileged place to the tradition, stories of spiritual experience, the history and concrete norms and rules of our religious congregation. These traditions, stories, and norms are concrete expressions of the aim and mission and scope of the common vocation. They are fairly explicit and precise. They bring the members one step closer to discerning the concrete will of God here and now. These traditions and norms are not for everyone, but we give them a privileged place in our discernment because they flow from the common commitment to which we have pledged ourselves.

In our listening, we also give a privileged place to the voices of our fellow religious, who share the same call and the same commitment. For reasons best known to God alone, we live here and now, with these concrete people, who have among them a sense, a feel, a connatural understanding of the meaning of the common vocation. What they have to say may often be hard to hear, because it is often particularly challenging. And we often wonder why God chose them (or ourselves) anyway. Yet in loving providence God has placed us together with these people. Their voices should exert particular influence in our discernment. Here we discover the valid sense in which we can speak of "obeying the community." This is an obedience in the sense of "listening." What the community has to say should be particularly significant for our discernment process. We do not obey the community as if the community itself were an institutionalized authority or a personal guru. But we should listen with special care to the words, hard or easy, which our fellow religious address to us.

Finally, in our listening as members of a religious congregation, we give privilege to the voice of those designated to bear the institutionalized authority of the congregation and constitute its recognized spiritual leadership. This is what has been traditionally emphasized in discourse about religious obedience. Religious have thought of these designated authorities as "mediators" of God's will. There is a sense in which this idea is completely true. Normally, the voice of those in positions of authority is in harmony with what we hear from all the other voices we have just been detailing. Even though those charged with institutionalized spiritual leadership are surely fallible, their voice carries special weight because of their responsibility to maintain and channel the unity of the congregation in pursuit of its common end and vocation. Religious listen to them with particular care and normally act on what they say, because of the conviction that the deep will of God is a oneness of mind and heart in the pursuit of the common charism.

We should expect quite rarely to find such discord among all these voices that we would have a real case of conscience and be pulled in diverse directions without any clarity in our effort to do God's will. We are often pulled in diverse directions, but the sources of the pulls are usually human weakness and selfishness rather than conflicting interpretations of the will of God for us here and now. Such conflicting interpretations are possible but probably not too frequent.

ON NOT TAKING OURSELVES TOO SERIOUSLY

It might be good to end on a note of not taking all this with excessive seriousness — especially not taking ourselves too seriously.

As we said at the beginning, the will of God for me here and now always remains a mystery. Obedience is a faithful listening, but I should always maintain a little healthy distrust of my clear-headedness and inner freedom in the process of discernment. The fact is, I may often be wrong. One of the reasons for giving so much weight to the role of institutionalized authority is simply to create some kind of unity among good people who often have conflicting ideas.

On a deeper level, we should not allow ourselves to become obsessed on this point, because we know that God is above all a savior. Authority and obedience are important ways we have of trying to be faithful to the will of God here and now. But our human limitation, weakness, conflictual motivations, and downright perversity are so pervasive that we often fall short of the mark. It is then that it is particularly consoling to know that God is above all One who brings the best out of evil and preserves all the good and beauty that exists in our life, even though it is mixed in with much that is not so good and beautiful. Our pursuit of the will of God will always remain flawed and mysterious.

We must do our best with the authority (life-giving power) and obedience (listening power) that we have, and then leave the result in God's hands.

If we can live with that confidence, God will be able to use us fully as instruments for the accomplishment of divine purposes.

CHAPTER 6

IN THE HEART
OF THE CHURCH

Mission and Ministry

The vast majority of Catholic religious are members of "active" communities. Much in the structure of our community life is geared toward empowering and facilitating our ministries. Our vitality is closely related to our sense of mission.

A key motivation for most of us in joining our communities was our desire to serve people and thus take part in the work of the church. Mission remains a focus of strong opinion and intensive reflection; there is probably no subject on which today's religious have stronger feelings and convictions.

For most of us, mission is much more than an abstract idea. It inspires and motivates us, has the potential to free our minds from limitations which human fears place upon our vision. It gives us a healthy sense of urgency.

Today I am convinced that a dynamic sense of mission will be powerful in renewing our vitality and dedication, in attracting new people to join us, and in creating a sense of vibrancy, enthusiasm, and joy in our personal and community lives. A powerful sense of mission takes us out of any self-absorption into which we might be tempted to fall and propels us into energizing service to others.

THE CONTEXT OF OUR MISSION TODAY: A TIME OF TRANSITIONS

And yet we religious, on whom the whole apostolic focus of the church so long fixed, are not always sure how we fit in today. A certain lethargy has overtaken some of our traditional ministries. Our very success has spawned imitators, and at times we no longer feel very necessary. Some of our traditional work does not easily lend itself to solidarity with the poor and the oppressed.

Moreover, our times are witness to a burgeoning gamut of ministries within the church. The laity is awakening to a new sense of responsibility. Much of this energy comes from Vatican II, much from the evolving culture around us. The church today is perhaps growing in an apostolic spirituality that expresses concern for the world and all its peoples. We religious can no longer look on ministry as "our" domain.

Transition can be exhilarating, but also sometimes discouraging. It can lead either to breakdown or to new life. The breakdown becomes evident when unassimilated change, whether in culture as a whole or in our personal lives, makes us turn in upon ourselves. Some call our era an "age of narcissism." We become preoccupied with ourselves, our problems, our adjustments. Such self-preoccupation is mirrored in the literature we read and the television we watch.

But positive forces are also at work within our transitional culture. Seeds of new life are beginning to take root, and our challenge is to nurture and develop them into a dynamic mission-oriented thrust. While the process is still going on, we feel the stretching and tension within ourselves. In the midst of our transitional times there are new energies waiting to come forth—waiting for our courage and creativity. We all share some responsibility for our future. We need to be co-creative with the Lord of history, not just passive.

A CATALOGUE OF CHALLENGES

What should we be doing in these transitional times? This fundamental question underlies today's thinking about mission.

At stake are challenges facing everyone serious about church mission in this era since Vatican II. The following are just a few of the principal questions and challenges:

1. Most of our communities still need to come to a clear sense of priorities or "preferential options." These priorities and options need not exclude other activities and ministries, but they give us a focus for training and decision-making and a yardstick for evaluation. The Latin American church of today is famous for its preferential option for the poor and for youth (Puebla). This option has invigorated religious in that part of the world and galvanized many of their best energies. The same is happening, perhaps with less fanfare, in South Asia. But other options and priorities need to be considered in other parts of the world, perhaps in some places "re-evangelization" or "the empowerment of the adult laity" or "the deeper evangelization of the middle class." Each cultural area and certainly each religious community needs to have a sharp and energizing sense of its key thrusts. When this is lacking, we seem rudderless and tend to focus only on internal problems.

2. Nearly every religious community began as a movement of lay people who wished to bring new life into the church. Over time we have come to think of the laity more as objects of mission than as fellow apostles. How can we once again work as partners with the laity at a common mission for the good of the whole church? In areas rich in religious and clerical vocations, like Africa and Asia, this is a special challenge.

3. We need a more vivid global sense, an awareness of the universality of mission. Our church must no longer be centered in the long-established furrows of Europe and North America, but genuinely be a world church. In their history most religious communities have identified very well with certain ethnic groups of people, but have had difficulty in transcending ethnicity and inculturating in other groups. How can we enter more effectively into the lives of other groups, especially those that are neglected, such as ethnic minorities and oppressed communities? How can we enter selflessly, as learners and not only as competitive outsiders, into the rich and complex world of the other great religions?

4. The founders of most apostolic religious communities gave particular stress to work with the poor and less privileged sectors of society. Time and historical circumstances have inevitably led many of us to a closer identification with the middle and affluent classes, even in poor countries. But the option for the poor is no longer optional. We must not trivialize it by vague references to spiritual poverty that allow us to sidestep a piercing reexamination. We cannot be genuine church ministers and ignore the pressing calls of today's poor. How can we minister effectively to the needs of the poor? How can we evangelize the middle class in such a way as to challenge consumeristic habits and motivate affluent Christians to take greater responsibility for the world's poor?

5. Many of the situations in which we work are designed in the first place to meet people's secular expectations (their desire for education, social service, counselling, etc.). And yet our deepest aim is not to be professionals in the fields of social service, health, education, or psychology. It is easy to get caught up only in meeting secular expectations and not relating them integrally to our sense of Christian discipleship. Even when we labor among those who follow other religious faiths or those who accept no religion and are unlikely to do so, we need to understand our service as a witness to the faith we find in the gospel. Fully respecting the freedom and sensitivities of those we serve, we must make sure that our commitment grows out of our faith.

6. In many parts of the world we religious are in numerical decline. Even in other areas, a new aligning of priorities often means that we cannot continue doing all we have been accustomed to do. How can we maximize effectiveness? Should we follow a policy of withdrawal and regrouping, or should we find better ways of having a significant influence with fewer numbers? Is there a limit below which there is not a sufficient "critical mass" to exert a meaningful influence in a given situation?

7. Some ministers stress person-to-person ministry, helping people cope and grow, aiming at self-awareness, integration between life and religious experience. Others focus more on

transformation of society, social justice, development, liberation, and solidarity with the oppressed. These two emphases are compatible in theory, but how can we unite them in fact? How can the social ministers and the spiritual ministers communicate and work effectively together?

PATTERNS OF RESPONSE

The ways each of us responds to the apostolic challenges of our transitional times reveal significant differences in our ideas about the role of the church and religious communities in our modern world.

Some feel that changes in the world, for the good or the bad, need have only minimal impact on religious life and mission. For these, religious life is a state of perfection, bound to its unchanging essential elements. We should remain faithful to our historic works, which continually prove their worth, and ride out the winds of change in our age of transition, hoping for a return to the classic Catholic synthesis, which will reassert its validity.

Others see the relationship between church and world as pre-eminently a critical one. Our thrust as religious should be prophetic, announcing the Good News and denouncing the evil from which it saves us. This stance logically leads to a counter-cultural lifestyle, a radical attitude in ministry, and a willingness to enter into controversy, sometimes almost a relish for it, in the name of the gospel. Those who adopt this stance call for a severe re-examination of our corporate ministries, a readiness to withdraw from many of them, and a pioneer thrust to meet new challenges today.

A third group stresses the positive action of God in today's world. For them, our task is mainly one of integration, inculcating respect and love for creation, an incarnational sense of the goodness of today's world, and a progressive outlook. These people feel that the church should overcome its "fortress mentality," take on the great advances of our times in such areas as participative decision-making, the use of technology, and the heightened awareness of equal rights. In our ministries, this group tends to call for adaptation, energetic and progressive leadership, and a pragmatic approach toward maintaining traditional works and initiating new ones.

Each of these positions surely contains something of the truth. Our stances are probably influenced as much by age, temperament, and experience as by analysis and discernment. We need to recognize the different truths each of us has to contribute to the whole picture. We also need to be willing to dialogue and collaborate in order to establish clear plans of action for our communities, responding to the providential signs of the present and incorporating the varied facets of the truth about ministry for us here and now.

SOME ASSUMPTIONS ABOUT MISSION

Even when we take into account all our differences, most of us share some significant assumptions about our ministries today. These assumptions are full of implications for reevaluating, stimulating creativity, and redefining approaches.

1. We need to root ourselves in genuine apostolic spirituality and to understand the incarnational consequences of our apostolic vocation. Apostolic communities have sometimes taken on too many characteristics of an enclosed and cloistered life.

2. Our life of strict "separation from the world" is over. This has nothing to do with privacy or the spirit of prayer and reflection. It does have everything to do with being part of the place where we live, the local church, even the neighborhood. It refers to an attitude and an interest, a willingness to participate in the life of those around us.

3. Education and formation are life-long ventures. Some of us find ourselves outdated and fearful, or underused, employed below our capacities. This speaks to a need for updating, continuing education, ministerial evaluation, and the willingness to take responsibility for our personal life—a holistic approach to health, work, and community.

4. All ministries need to be properly adapted to today's life situations. We cannot minister in a vacuum. We need to reassess

and study the situations (poverty, racial and communal discrim-
ination, family breakdown, social and economic factors) which
affect the people whom we serve. This study, in which the people
among whom we minister should be fully involved, will help us
raise our consciousness of the context of our ministries.

5. Creativity and the courage to act are of the essence today.
Creativity is a possibility for every person. We can all go beyond
the routine and limits of our daily life, beyond what we are now
doing. To be creative usually means to live with anxiety and
defenselessness, but it brings about new possibilities for meaning. Some of the most creative moments in history have come
out of chaos—whether private, spiritual chaos or public, global
chaos.

6. Collaboration is a requirement of the church's future. Our
formation programs, initial and continuing, must emphasize, not
separation and corporate self-sufficiency, but involvement with
the needs of the local church and a collaborative stance with
other groups of men and women. Church needs will increasingly
push us in this direction. We must be prepared for this way of
acting and open to the demands it makes on our personal lives
and communities.

SOME BASICS OF MISSION: THE SERVICE OF FAITH

Whatever the truth about societal change and our personal
attitudes, about the challenges we face and the assumptions we
share, some basics remain constant for all mission and ministry.
Rethinking basics always has a way of renewing our vision. In
trying to capture some of these basics, I will probably not be
inclusive enough to fit every charism and surely not precise
enough to communicate the corporate richness of each community. But I hope that most religious may find some stimulation
in the following reflections.

Every Christian mission aims to be in some way, directly or
indirectly, at the service of faith. Some religious groups exist for
"primary evangelization," proclaiming the word of God to people who have not heard it before, pioneering church life where

it does not yet exist, building up new structures of the church. Other groups give greater emphasis to the pastoral work of providing opportunities for the expression of faith to those who already believe, allowing people in whom the faith has already taken root to maintain and exercise their faith. Still other groups take an educational approach to faith, building on pastoral care and seeking to form active and committed Christians.

Whatever our approach, today I think all of us religious need to ask whether we really put our time, energy, money, dedication, and all our other resources sufficiently at the service of faith. If we can't do everything in our institutions, do we really put a priority on the development of faith life? What are our concrete programs? What is the quality of our religious ministry in our schools? How is lay faith community evolving in our parishes? How much interest, time, and energy do we give to the formation of faith life among our lay co-workers, among parents, friends, parishioners, students — all the varied publics among whom we minister? Even when these profess other religions and ideologies, we need to be at their service in exploring and developing values to live by.

What can we do in order to give a higher priority to the service of faith? Our schools, parishes, hospitals, retreat houses, and other institutions will rise or fall in the long run on the seriousness with which we take this fundamental thrust. If we let it be only lip-service, without concrete programs, we will eventually lose our conviction that a given work is worth doing. And we will certainly never attract idealistic young people to come join us in this work if they don't see us really dedicated to our professedly fundamental goal.

COMMUNITARIAN ACTION AND CORPORATE MINISTRY

Most religious communities give high value to ministries that are undertaken in common by the members as a corporate expression of their sense of mission. Even if some individual members work alone, the community aims to be a unified apostolic group which supports, guides, and evaluates the work of each.

This communitarian stress is both a limitation and a source of strength in mission. The church needs dedicated individuals — for example, good pioneers who can go out and make new beginnings entirely on their own. But it also needs people who can create a sense of community, who can dedicate themselves to the demands of corporate ministry. Christian communities have a better chance of forming themselves in faith through mutual interaction; in turn they will be apt to attract and form other faith communities. Living and working together in community is a witness, repeating the example of the primitive Christian community of Jerusalem.

In the post–Vatican-II church we need to enlarge the traditional concept of corporate ministry to embrace the idea of collaboration with lay ministers. Sharing the Christian, ecclesial thrust of the work with the lay workers at our side should be one of our chief concerns, because we cannot achieve the mission alone, working only as religious, but even more because the church has called all its members to responsible and collaborative ministry. This aspiration will become a reality only if we take it on as a conscious concern.

Some of our failures, our inability to get good projects off the ground, are caused by difficulties in the community spirit. Usually we are competent, even very competent, in our individual tasks within our schools, parishes, and other centers. Most of our pain, anxiety, and frustration come from a weakness in supporting one another, in pulling together to overcome obstacles.

When we work as small teams, this difficulty can become very evident. If a group of three or five or seven of us is not able to work harmoniously and support one another, the mission we share will very probably fail. People will perhaps admire our individual competence, but our corporate inability to "get it all together" is bound to be our eventual downfall. Even where larger numbers are involved, the problem is very much the same, although the presence of sheer numbers may somewhat mask a lack of unity, at least for a while.

Today's emphasis on trying to understand one another, on affirmation, team administration, dialogue, and faith-sharing in community is emphatically not "navel-gazing" or "nesting" in a warm, supportive atmosphere. It is an essential mark of a collaborative approach to mission.

Do we really support one another in life and ministry? How can we overcome obstacles to such support? Do we broaden our corporate spirit to include the lay ministers with whom we work? Can we honestly say that the people we know see in us some glimmer of the first Jerusalem community? I am sure that the long-range viability of each of our corporate works depends very greatly upon the answers to these questions.

Despite our strong heritage as religious concerning community, this thrust is challenging today. Individualism is characteristic of our times, and we are tempted to be "lone rangers" in ministry. Strong community life — communities of relationship and not only of observance — and effective corporate ministry demand sacrifice and a deep corporate spirituality.

AN EMERGING AWARENESS:
THE SOCIAL DIMENSIONS OF FAITH

The awareness of social dimensions has always been implicit in religious ministry. It motivated founders and reformers to shape their congregations in response to the social needs of their times. But today social consciousness has become a key element in reflection about church mission.

The call to greater awareness of the social dimension of our ministries is not principally a call to enter new ministries, although it surely implies some of these. Most of our traditional ministries — education, health-care, preaching, social service — have great potential for a transformative effect on society. We can realize this potential more fully if we attend carefully to the impact we have on the world around us and the impact that world has on us. Ministry to individuals is not opposed to ministry to society; they are integrally linked in the mission of the church. Becoming more aware of this linkage is a special grace of our times.

For some reason, social consciousness in ministry seems to

frighten many of us today. I believe we are doing many of the right things, but justice and peace seem threatening to many religious when they reflect on corporate mission, as if they had a bad conscience.

We could do better, I believe, if we calmly worked at integrating a concern for the poor and the victims of oppression wherever we are. Our danger is to shy clear of this issue so long that it finally becomes overpowering and forces us to abandon some of the real opportunities in our current works.

The point is not only direct involvement with poor people. Such involvement is a gift that will enrich anyone who receives it. Jesus was directly involved with the poor and oppressed of his time, but he also spent much of his time with the rich and powerful. The significant point is that his interaction with the rich and powerful, as recorded in the gospels, challenged their good will and their incipient faith to develop a social conscience. His preaching did not stop at personal piety and individual morality. His ministry included "comforting the afflicted" and "afflicting the comfortable."

Whether we are working with the poor or with those who are more favored, those in distress and misery or those in comfort and luxury, we need to look carefully at what we are communicating. Is it the "faith that does justice"? Are we helping our parishioners, students, and friends develop a social conscience?

And we need to look, calmly, confidently, humbly, at ourselves as well, to ask if we can improve the social dimensions of our practice of faith: what we are saying by our attitudes, the way we live and treat people in our institutions.

Much more could and should be said about the mission and ministry of religious today. These are only jottings in a notebook that grows with experience. More and more, we are aware today that mission is not merely something we do but something we are. It expresses a way of being in response to the Lord. A powerful sense of mission will open new paths to our future vitality as religious.

CHAPTER 7

LIVING IN TRANSITION

Spirituality and Diminishment

My move from the United States to Asia has enriched perspectives and called into question some previously held certitudes. It has also revealed some striking differences in challenge and in mood. In the next two chapters I will reflect on some dimensions of a spirituality that seems appropriate for each situation. Of course, it is neither possible nor desirable to maintain a rigorous distinction and artificial contrast on all points, since many gifts and difficulties are identical or similar in the two situations.

In this chapter I hope to share some reflections on the faith experience of Western religious today. Much of what I write here will probably be recognized and affirmed by Asian religious as well, but the over-all feeling and appropriate spiritual attitudes seem rather different between East and West.

Greatly simplifying, one might say that Western religious, living with a feeling of corporate diminishment, are called to a paschal spirituality which emphasizes purification and a readiness for certain kinds of disengagement; meanwhile, Asian religious, living amid expansive growth, are called to a spirituality of incarnation, immersing themselves much more deeply in their time and place.

It may seem unduly negative to use the word "diminishment" to describe the experience of Western religious. New opportunities for renewal abound, and we are learning much about collaborative attitudes, prophetic ministry, and the witnessing dimension of religious life. "Diminishment" is accurate only in describing the subjective experience of great numbers of us Western religious. Educated and experienced in a church that centered most of its ministerial focus on us, now living with aging and small numbers of younger members, we tend to feel a loss of vitality and a fear for the future of our institutions and communities. In this chapter I will argue that this situation is providential and full of reasons for hope. But the feeling of diminishment seems a necessary starting point because it is so obvious and so widely shared.

OUR RECENT PAST: A PASCHAL EXPERIENCE

The past twenty years we have lived through in the church and in religious communities can well be understood as a paschal experience. Collectively we have experienced the decline and death of much in our past. We are assisting at the transformation or rebirth of a new form of being Catholic and religious. Few would probably dispute this statement, but it is still not clear what kind of child this "new birth" will be.

Many are preoccupied with symptoms of decline and death, and with uncertainty and anxiety about what lies ahead. I am convinced that the challenge to faith and hope is to see our experience as a participation in the paschal mystery.

When Jesus underwent his death and resurrection, the church passed through a variety of stages of response. Initially there was anger, blame, and fear. The disciples were disheartened. They felt that the end of their movement had come, and they blamed someone—the Roman authorities, the leaders of the Jews, Judas, or whomever— for what had happened.

Soon the disciples and the nascent Christian community moved from feelings of anger and resentment to anxiety about the end of the world, which they considered imminent. They felt a certain sadness about what was happening, but a conviction that the end was near. There was initially little effort to enter the world of activity and transform it in accord with any Christian vision. The accent was on preparing for the end.

As time went on, though, the early Christian community became aware of the way in which the message of Christ was calling it to a new vision and a new commitment. The community organized itself in a more permanent fashion, and its focus shifted from looking backward with a sad longing to looking ahead and working for the coming of God's reign.

SOME STRUGGLES AND GIFTS

Our religious communities have passed through some parallel steps during the past twenty years. Once we began to realize and accept that our life was changing, that numbers were decreasing, that collective aging was setting in, many of us had as an initial reaction feelings of anger and blame. We looked for someone to accuse of the infidelity that we thought to be at the root of our situation. Mostly we laid the blame on personal infidelities, often on administrations, formation programs, theologians, and the like. Those of us who bore those responsibilities were often tempted to discouragement and not infrequently succumbed. All of us laid heavy burdens upon one another and sometimes tended to miss the goodness and dedication so evident in the lives of our fellow religious.

One of the graces of the past decade has been a passage out of this stance of anger and mutual blame. We seem to have, on the whole, a better appreciation and acceptance of one another. Trust and mutual support are stronger.

Healthy personalism seems to be growing. We emphasize the unique worth of persons and their value—one of the results of the post-conciliar renewal. But we also recognize our vocation as a call to integrate personal richness in a shared venture with others. We are learning to celebrate and support one another and at the same time to call one another to fulfill personal gifts in a communion of life and ministry.

In these post-conciliar years, most religious have taken important steps toward personal spiritual renewal. A heartfelt personal spirituality, a sense of God active in personal salvation history, seems to be growing.

Our communities seem more ready than they used to be to confront human obstacles to individual and corporate spiritual growth — tragic problems such as alcoholism, the kind of anger that poisons attitudes and outlooks, other neurotic and self-destructive patterns. Since religious are almost universally very idealistic people, they are naturally prone to the nemesis of idealists: frustration and cynicism. There is nothing sadder, no greater human waste, than a bitter, frustrated, cynical idealist. We seem to be helping one another more effectively to deal with this nemesis.

The reassertion of respect and appreciation has cleared the way for some important steps toward a common sense of mission. Many communities have begun to reevaluate ministries, make courageous and sometimes painful decisions about closing some works and opening others, and reconceptualize their sense of mission so that a common thrust may serve as a rallying sign and a focus of reflection for all the members.

SOME MOODS OF THE PRESENT

Despite the positive gains to which I have just alluded, the over-all mood of religious in Europe and North America is unsettled and insecure about the future of their communities. In the wake of the past two decades it is not possible to remain unaffected, spiritually, intellectually, emotionally.

Sometimes the temptation is to be "fatalistic," bitterly resigned to a situation in which we find it hard to perceive God at work. In this mood we regret times past, resent much of what has happened, but believe that little or nothing can be done about it. So we withdraw from involvement in the life of our communities, feeling that our contribution will make no difference. We see no corporate future.

Another mood is that of "preservation," in which we also

long for the better days of the past, but focus energies on trying to maintain or re-create those days. Skeptical of new trends in the church and in religious communities, in this mood we continue to involve ourselves but often feel defeated or discouraged because so many aspects of the style of religious life with which we were most comfortable apparently cannot be recaptured.

Still another stance is that of "updating," in which we seek to maintain the institutions and traditions that come from the past, but also work within the givens of the present and try to integrate into existing institutions and traditions new directions that seem to hold promise of continuity and effectiveness for the future. This is a positive, hopeful outlook, but it can also be very frustrating if we misread the signs of our times and try merely to update when a more radical transformation is needed.

A fourth stance stresses "innovation." When in this mood, we are enthusiastic about the winds of change and try to foster innovations. We seek to promote new approaches in community life, new works, and are eager to experiment with new directions. We see the future more in these new directions than in the preservation of traditional institutions and practices.

Occasionally some of us fall into still another mood, that of "iconoclasm." Wanting to be on the cutting edge of change, we reject much of the past and traditional institutions. We want a radically new community in a radically new church. We are impatient with the pace of change and, paradoxically like those who feel fatalistic, tend to go off in our own direction, perhaps with a small number of like-minded friends. We feel little hope for working with the givens of the congregation as it is today.

Finally, in the vortex of such contradictory moods, it is easy just to "drift." When we give in to this temptation, we do not manage to define a consistent stance for ourselves, and float from one stance to another according to momentary reactions and enthusiasms.

Each of these attitudes probably exists within almost every congregation. There is a kernel of truth in each. One of the great challenges today is for each member to appreciate and honor the kernels of truth that he or she finds least appealing.

But each of these attitudes is also only a partial truth. If we let ourselves settle exclusively into any one of them, we will become discouraged and angry, alienated from many good people who have dedicated their lives in community with us. We will be closing ourselves off to a grace that God has prepared for us.

A "CHURCH OF FEAR"?

Carlo Carretto has remarked that "the post-conciliar Church runs the risk of going down to history as the Church of Fear" (Carlo Carretto, *Summoned to Love* [Maryknoll, New York: Orbis Books, 1978], p. 11). I believe he has hit upon one of the besetting temptations of our times. For both old and young, progressive and traditional, the collapse or doubtful success of a certain type of Christianity—our preferred type, whatever it may be—is a temptation to withdrawal, pusillanimity, even bitterness.

We sometimes think it more satisfying to implement our private visions, alone or with a few like-minded associates, than to live and work in communion with other Christians. We may have fallen into the perennial human pitfall of believing more wholeheartedly in the visible than the invisible, more in our own brand of Christian institutions and our own style of community and prayer, than in God. We may also have lost sight of the good will and commitment of other religious. We may stand at a critical and uninterested distance from them. Loneliness, unhealthy indifference to others, and mutual distrust are the inevitable results.

Admitting the gamut of individual stances, I tend to think that the word "resignation" captures better than any other the pervasive attitude of most contemporary religious in Europe and North America toward their congregations. We seem to exist in a quiet but unenthusiastic acceptance of the current situation. For the most part, we are realistic and practical, but a little overwhelmed by problems that seem insoluble. Our hope is not energizing enough. We are alive but not very dynamic; realistic, honest, relatively patient, but a little apathetic, lethargic, not intensely creative.

Of course there are many creative individuals and groups, many dynamic personal and corporate accomplishments — but despite these there is too much talk of death, not enough of resurrection, too much of decay and not enough of transformation.

The image of Holy Saturday seems to capture some of our experience: hopes and loves shaken, a quiet, uncertain time, waiting for some new movement and wondering if it will come, knowing that it can only come from the Lord.

We must hope that this current mood is only a temporary way station on a pilgrimage. "Resigned perseverance" is not an inspiring way of life.

Some of the steps we have been passing through are typical of any grieving process. Grieving people usually begin in anger and blame, move on to bargaining and sad resignation. The healthy endpoint is confidence and eager anticipation of the new reality that lies ahead. The challenge of the present is to move ahead into such a graced and healthy attitude about the corporate life of our religious communities, even if it means a "death" or a radical transformation.

CREATIVE FIDELITY TODAY: BEYOND RESIGNATION

Most of our founders had acute and dark visions of their times. Yet their very act of foundation was an act of hope, not discouragement. They understood their time and place in the church and were energized by a new mission. Universally they urged their disciples to live in happiness and thankfulness, because they were witnesses to extraordinary gifts of the Lord. Generally they urged over-anxious followers to relax and enjoy the unfolding of God's providential work.

Fidelity within a religious congregation is a relationship with God and human persons maintained by active, energetic cooperation with grace. Personal relationships based solely on cool, dogged perseverance rarely go far.

It is challenging to maintain such a covenant-like relationship throughout a lifetime. Vows would be meaningless if their object were consistently appealing and stimulating. Vows support our fidelity in moments of weakness; it is thus that they can lead to depth in maturity and fervor in love.

CHOOSING LIFE

The challenge at present takes the special form of the call to believe in God's promise to be present to us individually and collectively. God is undoubtedly calling us today to major transformations, but we know that God ultimately wills life. To live in that faith and hope is to be creatively faithful in our days.

If we allow the mood of resigned depression to settle in a dominant way over our future, we will not be able to see God at work creating new life. If we passively wait for others to set the conditions for vibrant religious life, the chances are that little will happen and we will gradually succumb to discouragement. Whether or not we remain "on the books" as members of our congregations, this kind of existence will not realize the potential of the grace given us in a religious vocation.

Today the great need of religious congregations is for members who are willing to give themselves unreservedly and with priority, in "good times and bad, in sickness and health, for richer or poorer." Without members who give such priority to their religious commitment, it might be better for the congregation not to continue. With the help of such members, we will be able to move beyond resignation into the hopeful anticipation of God's new gifts for the future.

We are being called to choose life for the future. This implies the need for transformation, not merely detailed adaptation or slow, incremental change. The ability merely to "cope" no longer suffices. The issue is not how to solve our problems, but how to enter wholeheartedly into this call for transformation.

A key focus for choosing life is a sense of urgency about mission, about what needs to be done in the church and world. Too much "futuring" is a luxury. Perhaps we need to learn more to leave the future and questions about corporate survival to God. We are not in control of our destiny; God is. Meanwhile we must be about meeting today's needs, doing something creative for church life in the here and now. Our task is to choose life for today, not to worry about forever. As individuals, each of us will die, but we have a lot of life and many tasks to accomplish before then.

RENEWED FOCUS ON SOME BASICS

One concrete way to choose life today involves a new focus on spirituality and community.

In post-conciliar times, we religious have attempted to integrate quite a gamut of new values and attitudes. In some cases, there has been admirable success; in others the integration remains more doubtful. The very attempt to integrate so much may have tended to blur a sharp focus.

For example, over these years religious congregations have become very good at the verbal level in articulating and explaining their ideals, charisms, and spirituality. Such articulation is meant to reinvigorate commitment. But too often "the power does not get to the wheels." We recognize and affirm the beauty and the values of the Christian life in our varied traditions, but we are busy about so many other things that we do not really let its power penetrate our lives.

A renewed focus would give priority of place to prayer, reflection, study of the spiritual life and the charism. The deepest motivation for becoming a religious is a certain fascination with God and the things of God. But as we pursue a variety of other objectives, our focus sometimes blurs and we do not give sufficient peaceful attention to the power of that primary motivation. Of course the forms and methods of prayer and reflection must adapt to the world in which we live. We need to be less cloistered and private, more prone to share with others. But adaptation of prayer life is a call to a greater steeping of ourselves in spirituality, not an excuse for easygoing neglect.

Another example of the blurring of focus: attitudes toward community life. We have become eloquent, perhaps sometimes romantic, in our praise of the joys of community. Sometimes ideals may be impossibly high for a group of normal people. And in fact we have often focussed on so many other objectives — most of them very good in themselves — that community life takes a secondary place.

We want an excellent community life, but we want to be able to plug into it when we are free from our other interests and obligations. We want someone else to make sure that good community happens. We are not so ready to take the responsibility, to enter into the free interdependence with others that makes community truly life-giving.

Sometimes our other interests and obligations arise from ministry, sometimes from family, friendships, hobbies, academic and professional pursuits. Any healthy life has to be a balance of many elements, but experiential community often suffers by being given a low priority.

Again, such a renewed focus on community will not restore past forms. Communities of apostolic religious today are busy places, and we are often called to invite non-religious to share in their dynamism. The new mode of community life will be less a closed circle of the vowed, more an open family reaching out to many. But this area of experiential community living needs particular attention. Jejune, ritualistic ways of being in community will not communicate the Lord's message.

To grapple sincerely and as corporate bodies with such a refocusing of priorities is one of the most important ways for religious to choose life at the present time.

A NEW RELATION TO THE LAITY

Today is a new age for lay Christians. Their very presence and active participation in ecclesial life sharpens the meaning of the vocation to be a member of a religious congregation. It is also a call to close collaboration, to work increasingly at their side, not to look upon them as mere "auxiliaries" or second-class "collaborators."

It is imperative today that we religious become participative and collaborative in our sense of mission. Too often we have looked upon the laity as passive sharers in our spirituality and mission, ourselves as the active force. The future of religious communities, I believe, lies in a much broader sharing of the life of these communities in the closest manner with lay people.

Lay Christians should be seen as bearers with us of a common ecclesial mission. What would mission statements look like if they were not simply descriptions of the efforts of groups of religious but expressed the thrust of larger groups of people, of differing lifestyles, who share a common vision and heritage? What kind of corporate commitments could be made by such consortia of religious and laity? At the present, how can we further develop programs of partnership to move in this collaborative direction?

Much of the vitality of religious congregations in the future will probably depend on the answers we find to questions of this sort. To ignore or avoid them is to duck the challenge of creative fidelity as religious today.

THE CALL TO HOPE AND LOVE

Above all, the Lord seems to be calling us religious, at this crucial moment of history, to hope and love. This call is issued to us in the face of pervasive temptations to discouragement and alienation. It is addressed not only to individuals but also to communities.

Hope is not the same as optimism, and love is not the suppression of differences or the pretense that there are no problems and failings. Rather, they are the attitudes of people who know that God is at work. We can live in hope and love only if we are so free and so secure in God's love that we can devote our best energies to the service of the kingdom.

To live in hope and love is a challenge to every class of religious today.

To youthful members, the challenge is to dedicate their lives and futures without total surety, to risk and be patient while their inarticulate strivings gradually take on form, and to be willing to learn from the grace working in the corporate heritage and the community elders, to give over to the Lord's control the future destiny about which they naturally feel anxious.

To the many entering new ministries, whatever their age, the challenge is much the same: to focus on the clear elements of the Lord's new call, to emphasize the essential dimensions of the charism, to collaborate with others, and to be free enough to accept feelings of success or failure as the Lord sends them.

To the majority of us, at work in long-standing ministries, the challenge is to take up with joy the task of reexamining, setting priorities, refocussing energies, patiently discerning directions. In the process we may be impelled to let go of some cherished elements of our activity, yet the reward of the renewed sense of mission can be great. Taking up a new call within traditional works, we will be able to discover a new freedom and a new sense of humility, as we experience the Lord, more than our own efforts, leading us.

To the elderly, the challenge is above all to be gracious in accepting the blessings and gifts that have come through a long life. Older religious have been deeply involved in the graced history of the past. Their call is often to let go, to trust other members to take over, and to see change in some form of ministry to which they have long been devoted. This call is not a defeat, but one of the blessings of success. They have done their work well, brought the church to a new stage in its life, and the focus of energies can in some cases now shift in other directions. The elderly are challenged to trust that God will really be at work through the succeeding generations, even though they themselves can no longer be in the thick of things. God wants to lead them in new ways now, and prepare them for something greater than they have yet known.

Thus the challenge is pretty much the same for all: to let go of the anxious urge to plan our lives according to our private visions, and to trust in God's work in others, to strive to be one in heart and soul, and to let God lead us. With this attitude, hope and freedom will be ours in a new way.

NEW LIFE

It is my great hope that such love, freedom, and confidence will in the long run be the hallmark of our time rather than any temporary mood of discouragement or alienation.

At this turning point in the church's history there is an understandable sense of loss over some forms of beautiful Christian dedication and generosity that have faded a bit. But even more there is a great potential for creative and bold service to the enduring work of the gospel in the world of the twentieth and, soon, the twenty-first centuries.

We cannot predict exactly whether or in what form we will survive, how numerous we will be as religious congregations, or what precise forms the service of religious will take in the next age of the church. But we have God's fidelity as a promise that God will accompany us on our historic journey. Our task is not to determine in advance the shape of the future, but to take the steps required of us, each day, in trust that God cares much more for us and for our future than we ourselves do.

CHAPTER 8

IN THE HEART OF THE WORLD

The Inculturation of Religious Life

The spiritual opportunities and challenges of Asia are quite different from those of the West. The previous chapter was a distillation of two decades of vivid personal experience and a multitude of living contacts. In the current chapter I am necessarily more tentative, reflecting on ten years of occasional encounters and recent but brief impressions of full-time ministry in South Asia. Perhaps my observations, incomplete as they inevitably are, may make up in freshness and comparative consciousness for what they lack in depth and breadth.

UNIDIRECTIONAL HISTORY: A FAULTY ASSUMPTION

It is too often assumed in Christian circles that the religious evolutions of Europe and America will be repeated, perhaps with some dilution of impact and at an interval of a generation or two, in the rest of the world. Many presume that other cultures will inevitably come, in time, to adopt contemporary Western attitudes toward secularism and faith, tradition and innovation, individuality and communal rootedness — that these attitudes are simply the latest stage in a long and necessary path of historical development, through which all other cultures must pass.

These assumptions are far from self-evident. To expect a uni-directional history in all cultures is to ignore the way in which attitudes in the West have been formed by such peculiarly European experiences as the Reformation, the Enlightenment, and the Freudian era. Each cultural heritage is individual, with its own characteristics and collective historical memory, its own set of symbols, convictions, and significant relationships. None of the European historic experiences just mentioned could fail to create worldwide reverberations, but their effects have been less central and determinative for Asian, African, and other "non-Western" cultures, than for the one which gave them birth.

Elites in a number of Asian and African countries have been highly educated for some generations now in the modes of scientific, historical, analytic, and critical thinking that evolved in Europe and North America, and yet they still cling in highly significant respects to values and attitudes that grow out of their ancestral heritages. Their encounter with Western modes of thought has introduced significant cultural modifications, but these have tended in different directions than in Europe or America. Every culture is not fated to follow the same path of historical development, one based on the trajectory of "more advanced" Western experience. Similar historic causes will produce quite divergent effects, depending on the soil in which they are planted.

AVOIDING VICARIOUS SPIRITUALITIES

Thus, it cannot be taken for granted that the contemporary experience of religious communities in the West—an experience on which I have reflected in the preceding chapter—will simply be repeated elsewhere. The assumption of unidirectional history creates a certain sense of foreboding and cautious cynicism.

If we assume a unidirectional history, then there is only a limited need to assess the unique conditions of non-Western cultures and fashion spiritualities appropriate to them. If India will eventually reproduce European or North American conditions, we can wait to respond with a synthesis already worked out in the West. So a faulty assumption about history leads to a vicarious spirituality. Such a spirituality impedes openness to the grace of the present moment.

One of the functions of biblical prophets, Walter Brueggemann tells us, is to tell "what time it is," to recognize the signs and the locus of God's action at any moment in history (Walter Brueggemann, *The Prophetic Imagination* [Philadelphia: Fortress Press, 1978], pp. 53 and passim). If religious have a prophetic role, then their spirituality must vary in accord with differing times and places. To live in an invariable and homogeneous spirit, untouched by the opportunities and challenges about them, would be infidelity.

The foregoing is a truism with regard to differing times in history, but we are only beginning to realize its implications for differing places and cultures of the same era. Religious in each cultural area are called to discern the signs of their place, as well as those of their time, and to fashion their lives and ministry in response.

No one can be certain of the future, but the mood of knowing discouragement to which the assumption of unidirectional history gives rise is hardly an appropriate response to God's work of transforming a Eurocentric church into a world church. Religious in the Third World need to attend closely to their own experience and the richness of their contemporary culture in developing a spiritual response to our times. It would be one of the saddest of their many ideological imports from the West if Catholic religious were to adopt a vicarious spirituality, based on the experience of other times and places, instead of one that grows out of God's action today, here and now, in their midst.

INCARNATION AND INCULTURATION

It is impossible to say much about inculturation in the abstract. In what follows I will therefore focus on our situation in India. What, then, are some characteristics of a spirituality appropriate to Indian religious in our times?

At whatever aspect of Christianity we look, we have to admit that, still today, even in India, our tradition is deeply European. The classic Christian synthesis of thought, culture, and lifestyle was the result of a long series of encounters between the gospel message and cultural milieux: Jewish, Hellenistic, Roman, Byzantine, Germanic. Once this synthesis was attained and stabilized, however, it resisted similar encounters with other experiences. Especially in the long era after the Reformation and Counter-Reformation, when Christianity was first introduced to most parts of India, Christian discipleship tended to be identified with specific uniform European ways of thinking and speaking, living, relating, and organizing daily life. Each Christian group, Catholic or Protestant, tended to find its identity in a particular synthesis of European Christianity and to resist other modes as non-Christian. The integration of modes of life and thought from Asia or Africa or America was thought to endanger the essence of Christianity. Little distinction was made between the core of the gospel and its cultural trappings.

Religious communities exemplified this Europeanization to a remarkable degree. Dress, diet, timetable, modes of address, types of work—all tended to copy the customs of the country of origin. Religious communities saw their life and mission as an effort to preserve an imported tradition more than to grapple with new experience on a foreign soil. The fact that, in spite of themselves, these religious communities contributed greatly to a gradual rooting of Christianity and an unacknowledged inculturation is a tribute to the pastoral sense of their members and the strength of the local cultures they met.

Today we recognize a conscious and effective commitment to inculturation as a demand of the gospel, linked to the incarnational stance which is the heart of the Christian mystery. Even in North America in recent years, the theme of indigenous theology, indigenous religious lifestyle, and the interfacing of Christian life and American culture have been high on the agenda of most thinking Catholics. These are certainly even more necessary themes for those of us who live in areas of non-European culture, as part of our passage from a European to a world church. Our Christianity is too often a flowerpot phenomenon, a beautiful foreign perennial blooming under the Indian sun, rather than a rooted native shoot. An incarnational and kenotic spirituality is the basis for passing over to a self-renewing reality.

Such a spirituality will transform all areas of our religious experience. It will lead us to a prayer life that integrates much of the wealth of Indian *sadhana* into Christian faith and inculcates a more contemplative, less activist form of discipleship. It will require a simpler, more stripped-down lifestyle, closer to that of the ordinary people who surround us. In our way of living together, it will lead us from the patterns of Western individualism to a deep Indian sense of community. It will cause us to review our living of each of the vows in the light of the exigent traditions of Indian non-attachment. In ministry, this spirituality of inculturation will lead us to the use of simpler means and to a deeper engagement with the spiritual quest of those we serve. In theological thought, it will prompt us to become learners in the school of Indian philosophy and spirituality, so as to enrich our own Christian heritage with the "seeds of the Word" that have been sown for centuries by Indian seers in their own soil.

INCULTURATION OF SIGNS AND SYMBOLS

A simple but quite demanding level of inculturation is that of signs and symbols. To the outsider in India, Christianity appears very European: a matter of large and intimidating buildings, efficient but impersonal institutions, foreign architecture, dress, and food. Gothic churches — English and French in inspiration — dot the landscape in the more Christian areas of India.

If our outsider happens upon a Christian worship service, he or she will probably find it inexplicable, incorporating an extravagant way of dressing, the use of esoteric symbols, a foreign mode of music and speech, and a set of personal attitudes and postures that convey no meaning. Being an Indian, this outsider will approach this phenomenon with respect and patience, will perhaps try to enter into it out of politeness, but will remain perplexed and unmoved.

Christianity is unique, but it should not remain foreign. We lose our Christian emphasis on incarnation and kenosis when we cling to the *nama-rupa*, the "names and forms" that speak only to a mind penetrated with classical Western culture.

Signs and symbols of religious reality are abundantly available in India, but adopting them is not easy for us. We have felt considerable prestige and a sense of identity through the acceptance of foreign signs and symbols. Today both our sense of mission and our authenticity as fully Christian and fully Indian require that we let go of alienating names and forms and accept those that surround us, just as Christians in the early church integrated symbols from their own hellenistic cultural environments.

INCULTURATION OF LIFESTYLE

Indian religious are deservedly noted for their simplicity of life and willingness to undergo privations in the service of mission. In this sense they remain close to their roots in Indian village life, which is characterized by an ability to live joyously with an absolute minimum of material possessions and comforts. Yet our living habits within Indian religious communities tend too much to reproduce a European, urban mode of life. Sitting on chairs, wearing shoes and Western garb, eating with cutlery, living in European-style dwellings—these are petty but telling examples of the Westernization that has long been taken for granted among church personnel in the subcontinent. The fact that we religious can get by with a minimum of these European trappings and that we are often able to revert to simpler modes when necessary does not efface our basic witness, in the eyes of most of our neighbors, to a life that is fundamentally European more than Indian.

It seems strange that the daily experience of religious life has come to be so identified with European customs and habits. No doubt the long-term presence of so many foreign missionaries contributed largely to this result. Unthinkingly, proper religious observance came to be identified, in the minds of religious themselves, with the adoption and faithful observance of European manners. Such manners are associated with wealth in India. Yet holiness is inextricably associated with poverty freely embraced in solidarity with the common people. Hence our European lifestyle here becomes an obstacle to the sharing of spirituality.

It is costly for us today to adopt habits of daily life more similar to those around us. The problem is compounded by the presence of so many of us in urban centers, themselves fairly Westernized in lifestyle. Yet the shucking off of European trappings of life can only offer a renewal and a freshness to our witness.

INCULTURATION OF THOUGHT-PATTERNS AND LANGUAGE

For centuries Christianity has existed in India alongside profound Hindu, Muslim, and Buddhist patterns of thought and language. Somehow geographic contiguity has not contributed much to mutuality and enrichment. Christians have, for the most part, continued to mirror European concerns and modes of thought and expression. Occasionally we decorate our discourse with an Indian trope or brighten it with an Indian concept. But we are only beginning to grapple with the opportunities and challenges of our situation at a meeting-place of world religions.

Each of the world religions is unique; a facile synthesis or syncretism leads only to the stale unity of the lowest common denominator. Yet each of the religions offers an enriching insight and some illuminating spiritual paths into the divine mystery that is at the core of human existence. Each is a "home of the spirit" and a "receptacle of the Word of God" (*The Church in India Today* [New Delhi: Catholic Bishops Conference of India, 1969], p. 107). As Christianity increasingly becomes a global religion, it can profit enormously from interaction with other patterns of religious thought and expression. India is a privileged place where the dialogue between Christianity and other world religions can be pursued not only at a high intellectual level but also at the level of ordinary life and everyday human reflection and discourse.

The result remains unknown, but it will surely be a form of Christianity that incorporates the thought and insight of Indian philosophy and Indian religious experience. As a Christianity that builds on the kernels of divine revelation that penetrate the historic experience of India, it will offer to world Christianity a unique and compelling form of expression. It will also be a Christianity that is able to speak on religious grounds to followers of other religions, to communicate to them something of its own experience of Christ in names and forms that they find more easily recognizable.

PASSING OVER TO AN INCULTURATED SPIRITUALITY

For us Christian religious to deal patiently and creatively with inculturation on any of these levels requires a high level of spirituality. We Christian religious in India are accustomed to a European environment and deeply appreciate its accomplishments, its comforts, and its etiquette. This environment has unconsciously become part of our identity as Christians. To undo some of the "Europeanness" of our lives, to accept Indian signs and symbols in worship, Indian styles of providing human services such as education and health care, Indian forms of building, dress, and food, to let go of our defenses against Indian modes of thought and expression, is to let go of a part of personal identity, to enter into a paschal experience not totally unlike that of Jesus who "emptied himself" in order to assume human experience.

It is therefore not surprising that some of us are resistant to inculturation. If we accept the presupposition of a unidirectional history and believe that Asian culture will inevitably come to adopt Western patterns, we can even justify our unwillingness to change by the comfortable conviction that we are in some way the wave of the future.

Such specious arguments are as much felt emotional responses as they are intellectual assessments. They are less to be countered by reasoning than by experience. Entering incarnationally into the richness of Indian life in its historic concreteness, with its unique signs and symbols, its lifestyles and thought patterns, we will be able to experience the difference of a rooted Christianity that speaks clearly and spontaneously, without explanation and rationalization, religiously and not just pragmatically, to ourselves first of all and also to the people around us.

PASSAGES IN INDIAN SPIRITUALITY

Appropriate spiritualities in both East and West call religious today to a paschal purification. For us in India, inculturation inevitably involves a letting go of comfortable and reassuring modes of existence and an embracing of what seems fearful and uncertain. It leads us to pass from triumphalism to humility, from institution to person, from Western wealth to Eastern simplicity.

Triumphalism is a real temptation. Despite our minority position, we Christians in India count great accomplishments and rightly claim a disproportionate influence on public life. Our religious communities are experiencing rapid growth and developing vast networks of service and influence. Our institutions enjoy considerable social prestige. Greater inculturation may threaten some of this distinctive prestige; in becoming more Indian, we may become less elitist, more vulnerable. The courage to enter more deeply and intimately into the life of the people may make us more recognizable as religious people, but at the same time more subject to evaluation and critique on the basis of our spirituality and our sense of God.

The passage from institution to person is universal in the Catholic church today. A priority on the value of each person, reinforced by the teaching of Vatican II, has regularly called into question the marvelous institutional expressions of Catholicism that the past two centuries have developed. This passage has particular importance for us in India, a country that relies far more on personal relationships and dialogic interactions than on fixed structures. As long as we conceive the mission of the church primarily in terms of managing institutions, we will fail to enter deeply into the hearts and minds of our people. We will continue to be regarded as dependable and admirable public servants, but hardly as witnesses of the Spirit. Even within our religious communities, we sometimes relate bureaucratically or hierarchically and fail to honor the uniqueness of God's dealing with each member. The passage to a more personalist stance does not so much require the dismantling of institutions as a replacing of accent and reordering of priorities. This passage will be particularly agonizing for us.

The passage from Western wealth to Eastern simplicity is a corporate expression of religious poverty. We still rely very much on the impressive means which generous Western benefactors make available to us. We are leaders in the importation of Western goods, services, and concepts. Those we serve may be eager for what we have to offer, but they generally fail to see much connection with any religious mission. If anything, they may see us as a threat to the austere traditions of Indian spiritual life. Inculturation will mean a letting go of some of our sources of success on the pragmatic plane.

Incarnation always seems to imply humiliation; as long as we stand outside the mainstream, we remain safe. A spirituality for incarnation is necessarily a spirituality that is willing to accept humiliation and failure, at least in the eyes of some.

REALIZING INCARNATIONAL SPIRITUALITY

The spirituality appropriate for us in India today calls us to let go of many sources of security and influence and to embrace a kind of life and ministry that brings us closer to the poor of the subcontinent, exposing us to their scrutiny and opening us to the abysses of their needs, spiritual and material. It is a spirituality that makes us willing to let go of external signs of identity that have given us a certain kind of success and to accept an inner identity anchored more exclusively in Christ and not so much in the trappings of Europeanization. We are much better at articulating this challenge than at realizing it in practice.

Of course, this incarnational and kenotic spirituality is not a totally new reality; many have already gone far in practicing it. It is the way to genuine spiritual depth in our environment, even though it requires so much of each of us.

In this chapter I have spoken as a relative newcomer and a fresh wayfarer in India, seeking to articulate some helps for authentic Christian spirituality in our situation. There is surely much more to be said, but I am convinced that a wholehearted entry into the spirituality of incarnation and inculturation will be a unique grace not only for those of us who live and work here, but for the whole Christian church. For our religious life is destined to a growth and a series of mutations in India which will in time enrich the entire Christian world.